The Problem of Religious Freedom

Woodstock Papers

Occasional Essays for Theology

PREPARED BY

Professors of the Faculty of Theology
Woodstock College, Woodstock, Maryland

EDITED BY

JOHN COURTNEY MURRAY, S.J.
WALTER J. BURGHARDT, S.J.

No. 7

THE NEWMAN PRESS
WESTMINSTER, MARYLAND
1965

The Problem of Religious Freedom

by JOHN COURTNEY MURRAY, S.J.

Professor of Theology
Woodstock College

THE NEWMAN PRESS

WESTMINSTER, MARYLAND

1965

★ Contents ★

The Problem of Religious Freedom

★ Introduction ★

In a recent address to a seminar of the United Nations on freedom of information Paul VI said:

As you know, the Church also is busy with a somewhat different problem but one that is not without affinity with the present object of your research. It is the problem of religious freedom. The importance and amplitude of the question are so great that it has claimed the attention of the Ecumenical Council. It is legitimate to expect the promulgation of a text on the subject that will be of great import not only for the Church but also for all those—countless in number—who feel that an authoritative declaration on the subject is a matter of concern to them.[1]

This essay may serve to illuminate the formidable difficulties that the problem itself presents. They arise from two general sources.

First, there is the variety of religio-social situations throughout the world, and the differences among political traditions and regimes, and the divergences in the historical experiences of the nations.

For instance, religious freedom has been an integral part of the Catholic experience in the United States; the institution is considered to have made a contribution to the vitality of the Church. Elsewhere, perhaps chiefly in Spain, the institution is alien; the very notion connotes a hated *Liberalismo,* pernicious both to the Church and to a cherished national religious unity.

Again, there is the more difficult problem of Christian communities in lands of non-Christian tradition and culture—Islamic, Hindu, Buddhist. A declaration on religious freedom might be understood to signify the will of Christians to constitute a "state within a state," and to withdraw from solidarity with the existent national community. The result might possibly be governmental legislation against conversion to Christianity, as well as severe restrictions on missionary activity. Opposition on Christian grounds to governmental policies is an accepted phenomenon in those countries in which government pretends to do no more than administer the affairs of society; it is considered a legitimate exercise of religious freedom. The case may be different in those countries in which government is undertaking the task of constructing the social order, in the name of an ideology of which government is the representative. In these circumstances, opposition, based on an appeal to religious freedom, might be considered disloyalty to the state.

Furthermore, there is the still more difficult problem of the Church in countries under Communist domination. Some conciliar Fathers are in favor of a strong condemnation of Communism, both as an ideology and as a regime, precisely in the name of religious freedom. Others are inclined to doubt the value or prudence of such a condemnation. Still others consider that it would do more harm than good. If the Council were to declare, explicitly or implicitly, that the atheist is not free to profess his ideology and to make it the basis of a socialist-materialist society, the retort might well be: "The freedom that you solemnly deny to us, we shall deny to you with equal solemnity and con-

[4]

siderably more effect." There is also the more general problem of the atheist himself, and the secularist too. If the Council were simply to say to him that he is the enemy of the common good and therefore cannot be granted freedom, it would reveal itself as insensitive to the religious problem of today, of which the atheist and the secularist form so large a part.

Finally, there is the problem of making a declaration on religious freedom that will appeal to the common consciousness of all men of good will and furnish the basis of a badly needed dialogue between the Church and the world on this acute and universal problem. The scope of the Council calls for a pastoral act, which will at once clarify the doctrine of the Church and also demonstrate her concern for human freedom in this perilous age of ours.

The second source of difficulty is the contemporary state of Catholic doctrine on religious freedom. The fact is that serious differences of opinion presently exist within the Church. The fact was clearly demonstrated by the variant reactions to the three draft texts submitted in succession by the Secretariat for the Promotion of Christian Unity. Nevertheless, there is general agreement on the necessity of reaching a consensus and on the means of doing so, namely, the freedom of the conciliar dialogue, and the willingness of the Fathers to rise above any sort of apologetic complex and to approach the problem in the spirit of genuine theological inquiry.

The purpose of the present essay is not to present any personal views of the author. The essay undertakes, first, to state with all possible objectivity the two existent views on religious freedom (in order to avoid prejudicial characterization, they will be called simply the First View and the Second View), and second, to institute a dialogue between them, presenting the objections that each has to the other. In this way it may be possible to formulate clearly and without confusion the real issues.

At the outset, it may be useful to state the central question that is in dispute between the two Views. It concerns the care of religion by government. The technical term or phrase "care of religion" (*cura religionis*) is a post-Reformation coinage. But the problem goes back to the days when the Church first emerged into public existence within the ancient Roman Empire. It is a political problem, because it concerns the competence of government with regard to religion in society. It is a juridical problem, because it concerns the functions and limits of the coercive power of civil law in the same regard. It is a theological problem, because it touches doctrines of faith, chiefly in ecclesiology. It is an ethical problem, because it raises the issue of conscience and of human and civil rights. Hereinafter it will be called the "constitutional question." The practical reason is that nowadays an answer to the question of public care of religion is customarily provided, in one sense or another, in the constitutional law of organized political communities.

★ 1 ★

The Two Views

The problematic of religious freedom is abstract and simple. It is constructed by two related questions—the moral question of the rights of conscience, and the constitutional question.

With regard to the moral question, three cases are distinguished. First, there is the conscience that is not only subjectively formed in accord with higher norms (*conscientia recta*), but also formed by norms that are objectively true (*conscientia vera*). This conscience, which is the Catholic conscience, possesses the fulness of religious freedom, because religious freedom is rooted in objective truth. It is a positive concept. It is the social faculty of professing and practicing what is true and good, as the true and the good are objectively proposed by the eternal law of God (both natural and positive), subjectively manifested by a rightly and truly formed conscience, and authentically declared by the Church. Religious freedom in this sense is the requirement of the dignity of the human person. As a rational and moral being, man is constituted in his proper dignity by his adhesion to what is true and good. This is the religious freedom that the Church has always vindicated in the face of persecution of the truth.

[7]

Second, there is the case of the outlaw conscience (*conscientia exlex*). It recognizes no norms higher than its own subjective imperatives. Therefore it possesses neither rectitude nor truth. Therefore it has no rights; it can make no claim to religious freedom. Again the reason is that religious freedom is rooted in religious truth.

Third, there is the case of the sincere but erroneous conscience. It is formed in accord with higher norms that approve themselves to it, but these norms are not objectively true, at least not with the fulness of truth (*conscientia recta sed non vera*). Its rights are defined in terms of a distinction between internal personal freedom and external social freedom.

The erroneous conscience is endowed with internal personal freedom. It has the right not to be forced to abandon its religious convictions and practices and not to be coerced into acceptance of the true religious faith, against its own subjectively sincere mandate. It also has a right to reverence and respect on the part of others, and others have the duty of paying it reverence and respect. The respect, however, is not owed to the erroneous conscience as erroneous, since no respect is due to error, but to the man in error who is still endowed with that measure of human dignity which is synonymous with internal personal freedom. The duty here is therefore of the order of charity; its proper name is tolerance.

Furthermore, internal personal freedom is extended to include the religious freedom of the family—the right of parents to care for the religious upbringing of their children and to provide religious teachers for

[8]

them. Finally, some affirm that internal personal freedom includes the right to public worship; others, however, deny this right, for the reason that a public act of worship is already an act of public propaganda.

The erroneous conscience has no right to external social freedom. That is, it has no right to public expression or manifestation of its beliefs in worship, witness, or teaching. In particular, it has no right publicly to propagate or disseminate its belief. The reason is that error has no public rights; only the truth has public rights, scil., rights to be exercised within society. Therefore the case of the erroneous conscience raises no issue of right in the strict sense, no issue of religious freedom in the proper sense. It raises only the issue of tolerance or intolerance. The erroneous conscience can claim no immunity from the repression of its external social manifestations by the public powers. This immunity, however, may be granted as an act of tolerance.

The constitutional question is solved by appeal to the same principle that governed the solution of the moral question, namely, that only the truth has rights, whereas error has no rights, within the public sector of society. This is the supreme juridical principle which controls the order of constitutional law and the action of the state. Whence it follows immediately that the public powers may never positively authorize the public existence of religious error. The legal attitude towards error can only be one of tolerance. On the other hand, the public powers have no right to violate the internal freedom of the personal conscience, or the freedom of the family, by compelling the profession or practice of any religion or ideology.

[9]

For the rest, the constitutional question is solved in terms of a distinction between thesis and hypothesis. The thesis states the ideal—the care of religion that constitutional law ought to provide, per se and in principle. The hypothesis states the concessions that may have to be made to circumstances—the care of religion that constitutional law may provide, per accidens and in view of circumstances.

The thesis asserts two general propositions. First, the state is bound not only on the natural law but also on the positive divine law whereby the Church was established. Therefore the state has the duty, per se and in principle, to recognize by constitutional law that the Church is a perfect society *sui iuris* and that it is the only religious society which has a right *iure divino* to public existence and action. Since Catholicism is, by divine law, the one true religion, it ought to be, by constitutional law, the one religion of the state. Whence it follows that no other religion may have, per se and in principle, a legal right to public existence and action within society. A religion that has no right to exist *iure divino*, can have no right to exist *iure humano*. Therefore, per se and in principle, all false religions ought to be "exterminated," that is, put beyond the bounds of public life and social action.

Hence the thesis affirms the legal institution of intolerance as the logical and juridical consequence of the legal institution of "establishment" (*unica status religio*). Together, these two institutions exhibit the ideal instance of constitutional law, the ideal solution to the constitutional question of public care of religion. The solution is internally consistent. The supreme juridical principle—the exclusive rights of truth—is transposed into the legal institution of the one state-religion. The obverse of the principle—the rightlessness of error —is transposed into the legal institution of intolerance. The special argument for this latter institution proceeds in two stages.

First, religious error *may* legitimately be repressed by law or by the police action of the state. Since error has no rights, no injury is done by this repression. The internal personal religious freedom of the erroneous conscience creates for it no external social freedom. Therefore the man of erroneous conscience cannot be considered reasonably unwilling to submit to the repressive action of the legitimate authority, the state. It is per se and in principle irrational to oppose the repression of what has no right to existence. Second, error *ought* to be repressed by the state. There are four reasons. First, error and evil are per se contrary to the rational and moral nature of man. Second, they are per se contrary to the common good of society, which is constituted by what is true and good. Third, they are per se injurious to the rights of others, especially their right to be protected from error and evil and to be left undisturbed in the profession of truth and in the practice of the good. Fourth, error and evil are per se a scandal, an occasion of moral wrongdoing and of defection from the truth.

This, in brief, is a statement of the thesis, the ideal, the solution to be given, per se in principle, to the constitutional question as a *quaestio iuris*. There remains the *quaestio facti,* the question of applying the ideal in practice. This question gives rise to the hypothesis. The

[11]

distinction between thesis and hypothesis corresponds to the difference between national societies in respect of the religious composition of the citizenry.

Certain nations are Catholic, that is, the majority of the citizens are Catholic; or, as some prefer to say, the nation has historically reached the social consciousness of Catholic truth; or, as others prefer to say, the tradition of the nation has been a tradition of national Catholic religious unity. In these circumstances the thesis applies, per se and in principle. Other societies, however, are not Catholic; the religio-social situation is pluralistic; Catholics are only a minority; Catholicism has not permeated the national consciousness. In these circumstances the hypothesis applies, per accidens, as a matter of fact. That is, the Church forgoes her right to legal establishment as the one religion of the state, with its juridical consequence, legal intolerance. The Church, however, gives no positive approval to the resultant constitutional situation. Per se the situation is an evil, but it may be regarded as a lesser evil than the evils which would result from application of the thesis. Therefore it may be tolerated, per accidens and in practice.

The supreme juridical principle of the exclusive rights of truth, and its pendant distinction between thesis and hypothesis, establish a rule of jurisprudence with regard to intolerance and tolerance. This rule prescribes intolerance whenever possible; it permits tolerance whenever necessary. (The degrees of legal intolerance will vary; the essential thing is that false religions should be denied public existence, action, and utterance. So too the degrees of tolerance may vary.)

The political criterion, whereby the issue of the possibility of intolerance or the necessity of tolerance is to be decided, is the public peace. Within conditions of Catholic unity, where dissidents are a small minority, legal intolerance becomes possible without disruption of the public peace. It is, in fact, a means toward the public peace. In contrast, legal tolerance becomes necessary within conditions of religious pluralism, where Catholics are a minority. It is in turn a means toward the public peace. The religious criterion is the good of the Church. Within conditions of national Catholic unity the good of the Church is served by intolerance; elsewhere, by tolerance.

The First View puts forward its answer to the moral question, and its consequent answer to the constitutional question, as true, certain, and immutable, not only in respect of the constituent principles themselves but also in respect of their systematization (*impostazione*). The basic systematic concept is the exclusive rights of truth. The whole system, especially the disjunction between thesis and hypothesis, derives from this concept.

Moreover, this First View is declared to be the doctrine of the Church, supported by magisterial authority. The document of primary and definitive importance is alleged to be the Allocution of Pius XII, *Ci riesce*. There are two reasons. First, Pius XII affirms the basic systematic concept of the First View: "That which does not correspond to the truth and the norm of morality has, objectively, no right either to existence or to propaganda or to action." [2] Second, Pius XII proposes a doctrine of tolerance, not of religious freedom:

[13]

"Not to inhibit it [error] by means of public laws and coercive methods can nevertheless be justified in the interests of a higher and greater good." [3]

Moreover, this doctrine is in continuity with Leo XIII. Thus, on the moral question: "Right is a moral faculty. Hence We have said—what needs to be repeated—that it is absurd to think that this moral faculty is granted by nature, impartially and without distinction, to truth and untruth, to decency and indecency." [4] Thus also, on the constitutional question and the issue of tolerance:

> Nevertheless, it is with a maternal judgment that the Church measures the heavy weight of human weakness; and she does not fail to note the direction being taken by events and opinion in this our age. For this reason, although she grants no rightfulness except to what is true and good, she is not unwilling that the public power should put up with certain things that are at odds with truth and justice, when it is a question of avoiding a greater evil or of gaining or saving a greater good.[5]

Other texts of the same tenor are adduced from Leo XIII. In addition, there is the catena of texts, beginning with Gregory XVI, in which the "modern liberties," especially freedom of religion, are condemned. Finally, *Pacem in terris* is considered to be simply a pastoral document, expressing the concern of the Church for the dignity of man. This concern is shared by the First View, in its defense of the right to internal personal religious freedom. For the rest, John XXIII leaves intact the doctrine of the duties and rights of the state in the order of religion, as presented by the First View. This doctrine is traditional and unalterable.

[14]

The supreme juridical principle of the exclusive rights of truth embodies an understanding of the medieval axiom: "Extra ecclesiam nullum ius." The thesis reproduces the sense of the medieval doctrine of the two swords, according to which the temporal sword is available "at the will and command of the priest" (*ad nutum et iussum sacerdotis*) for the protection of the religious unity of Christendom (*christianitas*) and for the extermination of heresy. The hypothesis states the sense of the medieval doctrine with regard to tolerance of Jews and pagans, their rites and beliefs.

Moreover, the First View stands in continuity with the doctrine of theologians during the post-Reformation religious conflicts. At that time, both Catholic and Protestant theologians taught the distinction between personal freedom of conscience and public manifestations of religious belief. In the latter regard, the state of the question was the same as it is today, namely, religious freedom in the civil order is the prerogative of the truth; error is to be treated with civil intolerance or tolerance, as the case might be. Moreover, in those days as also today, a sociological distinction was made. There were kingdoms and principalities within which unity of faith still prevailed, on the whole; the Reform had only begun to make inroads; its adherents were a small group, not well organized, not possessed of significant social or political power. Within these conditions of fact, the prince could exterminate the Reform, by measures of greater or less severity, without serious danger to the public peace. Hence the prince was obliged to proceed with the policy of extermination. In contrast, there were states within which the Reform

[15]

was already well established and organized; it already claimed a sizable number of adherents, even among the nobility; it was therefore possessed of social and political power. Within these conditions of fact, the extermination of the Reform was no longer possible without danger of civil strife. Therefore tolerance became necessary and the prince was permitted to grant it, as the lesser evil. Per se and in principle, the prince's duty to care for religion constituted him the custodian of religious unity; per accidens and in practice, the prince was permitted to tolerate a plurality of religions within his jurisdiction.

On the other hand, the First View rejects certain conceptions of public care of religion that were prevalent in former eras. It recognizes that the modern Catholic nation is not the medieval Christian commonwealth; hence it denies that the religious prerogative of the emperor is to be transferred without alteration to the public powers in the Catholic state today. It denies that public care of religion may be prolonged into a *ius in sacra* or a *ius circa sacra*. It also denies the *ius reformandi* of the prince and its pendant, the *beneficium emigrationis*. It denies that the prince, by reason of his political sovereignty, is a competent judge of religious truth and *custos utriusque tabulae*. It rejects the notion that the prince, although he has no right to compel or impose religious faith, has nonetheless the duty and right to compel his subjects to hear the true word of God and to enforce outward conformity with the official faith. It admits therefore, in principle, that certain kinds of external constraint are incompatible with personal freedom of conscience.

[16]

In these respects, and in others, the First View represents progress within the tradition, a clearer and less confused understanding of traditional principles— in particular, the distinction between the religious order and the political order, and the limitations of political sovereignty in the order of religion. However, the First View maintains that progress within the tradition ended with Leo XIII and the systematization of his doctrine by subsequent canonists. Catholic doctrine has reached its final and definitive mode of conception and statement. It has defined forever the ideal instance of constitutional law with regard to public care of religion. Many changes have indeed taken place in the world since Leo XIII; in particular, there is a wide demand for religious freedom as a personal right and as a legal institution. These changes, however, represent decadence, not progress. Their sole historical effect has been to create more evils that the Church must tolerate; hence the scope of tolerance must be broadened. For the rest, the ideal remains, transhistorical, unquestionable.

THE SECOND VIEW

The problematic of religious freedom is concrete and historical. Its construction begins with a scrutiny of the "signs of the times." Two are decisive. The first is the growth of man's personal consciousness; the second is the growth of man's political consciousness. They were noted, in their relation, by John XXIII:

The aspirations of the minds of men, about which We have been speaking, also give clear witness to the fact that in these

[17]

our days men are becoming more and more conscious of their dignity. For this reason they feel the impulse to participate in the processes of government and also to demand that their own inviolable rights be guaranteed by the order of public law. What is more, they likewise demand that the civil powers should be established in accord with the norms of a public constitution and that they should fulfil their functions within limits defined by it.[6]

The political consciousness, which is the correlate of the personal consciousness, is further described:

> Moreover, the dignity of the human person requires that a man should act on his own judgment and with freedom. Wherefore in community life there is good reason why it should be chiefly on his own deliberate initiative that a man should exercise his rights, fufil his duties, and co-operate with others in the endless variety of necessary social tasks. What matters is that a man should make his own decisions and act on his own judgment, out of a sense of duty. He is not to act as one compelled by external coercion or instigation. In view of all this, it is clear that a society of men which is maintained solely by force must be considered inhuman. The reason is that in such a society men would be denied their freedom, whereas, on the contrary, they ought to be inspired, by all suitable means, to find for themselves the motive for progress in life and for the quest of perfection.[7]

Man's sense of personal freedom is allied with a demand for political and social freedom, that is, freedom from social or legal restraint and constraint, except in so far as these are necessary, and freedom for responsible personal decision and action in society. Freedom, not force, is the dynamism of personal and social progress.

The common consciousness of men today considers the demand for personal, social, and political freedom to be an exigency that rises from the depths of the human person. It is the expression of a sense of right approved by reason. It is therefore a demand of natural law in the present moment of history. This demand for freedom is made especially in regard to the goods of the human spirit—the search for truth, the free expression and dissemination of opinion, the cultivation of the arts and sciences, free access to information about public events, adequate opportunities for the development of personal talents and for progress in knowledge and culture.[8] In a particular way, freedom is felt to be man's right in the order of his most profound concern, which is the order of religion.[9]

Therefore the Second View holds that, in consequence of the new perspective created by the growth of the personal and political consciousness, the state of the ancient question concerning public care of religion has been altered. Today the question is not to be argued in medieval or post-Reformation or nineteenth-century terms, scil., the exclusive rights of truth and legal tolerance or intolerance, as the case may be, of religious dissidence. The terms of the argument today are, quite simply, religious freedom. The question is to know, first, what religious freedom means in the common consciousness today, and second, why religious freedom, in the sense of the common consciousness, is to receive the authoritative approval of the Church.

The Second View addresses itself to the question in its new historical and doctrinal state. However, two schools of thought seem to exist with regard to the method of setting forth the Second View, which they nonetheless hold in common.

One school regards religious freedom as formally a theological-moral concept, which has juridical consequences, scil., within the order of constitutional law. The other school regards religious freedom as formally a juridical or constitutional concept, which has foundations in theology, ethics, political philosophy, and jurisprudence. The first school begins with a single insight—the exigence of the free human person for religious freedom. Only in the second instance does it raise what we have called the constitutional question. Consequently, within this structure of argument the political-juridical argument for religious freedom is secondary and subordinate to the theological-ethical argument. In contrast, the second school begins with a complex insight—the free human person under a government of limited powers. The constitutional question is raised at the outset; it is equally as primary as the theological-moral question. Consequently, the political-juridical argument for religious freedom is co-ordinate with the theological-moral argument. In other words, both religious freedom, as a legal institution, and constitutional government, as a form of polity, emerge with equal immediacy as exigences of the personal consciousness in its inseparable correlation with the political consciousness.

The differences between the two ways of stating the Second View are not irreducible. In any event, three difficulties are alleged against the first structure of argument.

First, the notion of religious freedom as a human right seems to appear as a piece of theological-ethical theory, arrived at by a process of abstract argument, in a vacuum of historical, political, and juridical experience. The methodology here is vulnerable, in that it seems to divorce the issue of the rights of the human person from its necessary social-historical context. In contrast, in the second school of thought religious freedom presents itself concretely, as both a human and a civil right, embodied in a legal institution, which forms a harmonious part of a larger constitutional order of freedom. This order, in turn, appeals for its validity to traditional principles of politics, legal philosophy, and jurisprudence, as these principles are vitally adapted to the realities of historical experience today. In this fashion, religious freedom as a human right is validated in the concrete, by a convergence of theological, ethical, political, and jurisprudential argument. This methodology commends itself as more in accord with the historical consciousness that ought to preside over all argument about human rights.

Second, the first school of thought runs the risk of "overtheologizing" the notion of religious freedom as a human right and as a consequent norm for the juridical order of society. The result might be to propose the legal institution of religious freedom as the "ideal instance" of constitutional law with regard to public care of religion. This ideal would then stand in conflict with the constitutional ideal proposed by the First View. In consequence, a false argument would be set afoot. Traditional philosophies of politics, law, and jurisprudence do not recognize any such thing as an ideal instance of constitutional law. By reason of the very nature of law, the issue of the ideal never arises. The function of law, as the Jurist said, is to be useful

[21]

to men. Necessity or usefulness for the common good —these are norms of law. Legal institutions can never fall into the category of the ideal. This risk of an idealization of religious freedom is avoided by the second school of thought, in which the relativities of history receive due attention.

Third, the first school of thought runs the risk of setting afoot a futile argument about the rights of the erroneous conscience. This argument may well be inextricable. In any event, it is irrelevant to the constitutional question. The simple reason is that the public powers are not competent to judge whether conscience be erroneous or not. The good faith or bad faith, the truth or falsity of conscience are not matters for adjudication by the civil magistrate, upon whom public care of religion devolves. This unnecessary argument is avoided from the outset by the second school of thought, given its complex starting point, the personal and the political consciousness.

An orderly exposition of the Second View can best be made by making the classic distinction between the question of definition or concept (*quid sit*) and the question of judgment (*an sit, cur ita sit*). Moreover, in the methodology here being followed, the conceptual question is twofold: what is religious freedom, and what is its correlate, constitutional government.

The Conceptual Question

The question, what is religious freedom, is not to be answered a priori or in the abstract. The fact is that religious freedom is an aspect of contemporary historical experience. As a legal institution, it exists in the world today in the juridical order of many states. It is not simply a question of understanding what religious freedom meant in the Third French Republic under the Law of Separation of December 9, 1905; nor of understanding what it meant under the Estatuto Real of 1834 in the reign of Isabella II. For the theologian, the instant conceptual question is to understand what religious freedom means today, in so far as it presents itself as an exigence of the personal and political consciousness of contemporary men. From this point of view, the following description can be assembled.

First, religious freedom is obviously not the Pauline *eleutheria,* the freedom wherewith Christ has made us free (Gal 5:1). This is a freedom of the theological order, an empowerment that man receives by grace. In contrast, religious freedom is an affair of the social and civil order; it is an immunity that attaches to the human person within society, and it has its guarantee in civil law. Obviously too, religious freedom has nothing to do with the statute of the member of the Church in the face of the authority of the Church, as if the Christian could somehow be free from obedience to the Church, which is absurd. Still less has it anything to do with the statute of the creature in the face of his Creator, as if man could somehow be free from the dominion of God, which is even more absurd.

Second, the adequate subject of religious freedom in its proper juridical sense as a human and civil right, guaranteed by constitutional law, is the body politic as such, the People Temporal—collectively, individually, and in their corporate associations. This follows from the very nature of constitutional law. The people are constituted a people *consensu iuris* (in the classic phrase), by their consent to a common law which touches all and is to be approved by all (in another classic phrase). Hence the people as such are the adequate subject of all the immunities and empowerments which the common law provides.

Third, the juridical notion of religious freedom is complex in its content. Within the concept it has become customary to make a general division between "freedom of conscience" and "the free exercise of religion" (this technical vocabulary goes back to the sixteenth century, and it is too late to change it now).

In its juridical sense, freedom of conscience is the human and civil right of the human person to immunity from all external coercion in his search for God, in the investigation of religious truth, in the acceptance or rejection of religious faith, in the living of his interior religious or nonreligious life. In a word, it is the freedom of personal religious decision. This freedom is essentially social. A man's religious decisions, however personal, are made in the social context of man's existence. In making them, a man has the right to be free from coercion by any human forces or powers within the social milieu. Society and all its institutions are obliged to respect this right and to refrain from coercion. By coercion, here and hereafter, is meant all manner of compulsion, constraint, and restraint, whether legal or extralegal. It includes such things as social discrimination, economic disadvantage, and civil disabilities imposed on grounds of religion. Today it importantly includes coercive forms of psychological pressure, such as massive propaganda, brainwashing techniques, etc.

The free exercise of religion is itself a complex concept. First, it is commonly understood to include a twofold immunity: a man may not be coercively constrained to act against his conscience, nor may a man be coercively restrained or impeded from acting according to his conscience. (The question of the limitation of this right will be dealt with later.) Furthermore, three aspects of the free exercise of religion are commonly distinguished.

Ecclesial or corporate religious freedom.—This is the right of religious communities within society to corporate internal autonomy. It is their immunity from the intervention of the public powers or of any social agency in the declaration of their own statute of corporate existence, in the determination of their own doctrine and polity, in their internal discipline and self-government, in the appointment of officials and in the definition of their functions, in the training and employment of ministers, in their communication with other communities and with recognized religious authorities in other lands. This freedom also includes the immunity of religious communities from employment by the public powers as *instrumentum regni*. In a word, this freedom is the corporate counterpart of personal freedom of conscience.

Here too is the appropriate place to locate the religious freedom of the family, the rights of parents with regard to the religious education of their children, and the rights of the religious school in relation both to churches and to families.

Freedom of religious association.—This includes, first, the right to immunity from coercion in affiliating, or in ending affiliation, with organized religious bodies; and second, the same immunity in the formation of associations for religious and charitable purposes.

Freedom of religious expression.—This is the right, both of individuals and of religious bodies, to immunity from coercion in what concerns the public worship of God, public religious observances and practice, the public proclamation of religious faith, and the public declaration of the implications of religion and morality for the temporal affairs of the community and for the action of the public powers.

The common legal and civic consciousness today recognizes that freedom of conscience and its corporate equivalent, ecclesial freedom, are freedoms *sui generis*. The first concerns man's personal relation with God, which is by definition an affair of personal freedom in a unique sense. The second concerns man's relation to God as lived in community, in accord with the social nature both of religion and of man himself. Hence the right to internal ecclesial autonomy is likewise *sui generis*. Finally, freedom of religious association, inasmuch as it includes immunity from coercion in the choice of one's religious affiliation, possesses the same quality of uniqueness as freedom of conscience and ecclesial freedom, to both of which it is directly related.

On the other hand, the personal or corporate free exercise of religion, as a human and civil right, is evi-

[26]

dently cognate with other more general human and civil rights—with the freedom of corporate bodies and institutions within society, based on the principle of subsidiary function; with the general freedom of association for peaceful human purposes, based on the social nature of man; with the general freedom of speech and of the press, based on the nature of political society. The exercise of these more general human and civil rights, whether personal or corporate, takes place in the public domain, and therefore it becomes amenable to regulation by the public powers, in accord with recognized and reasonable criteria. The same is true of the free exercise of religion, inasmuch as it is a civil right cognate with other more general civil rights. The question is to know the criteria which must govern the action of the public powers in limiting the free exercise of religion. This is the crucial issue in the constitutional question of public care of religion. We shall return to it later.

For the moment, it is to be noted that the free exercise of religion remains a freedom *sui generis,* even though it is cognate with other civil rights. The reason is that in all its forms it raises the issue of man's relation to God, as conceived by doctrine, affirmed by conscience, socially organized, and proclaimed in public utterance. In contrast, other civil rights have only to do with man's relation to other men or to society.

The foregoing analysis presents the answer which the contemporary consciousness, personal and political, gives to the first conceptual question, what is religious freedom. (There may be a difficulty about the proper classification of the three freedoms listed, but it is of

[27]

minor importance.) Moreover, the foregoing understanding of religious freedom is substantially in accord with the understanding contained in the pertinent declarations of the World Council of Churches.[10] The fact is of some importance for the ecumenical dialogue.

The second conceptual question, what is constitutional government, is likewise complex. For our purposes, which concern constitutional government as the political correlate of the juridical notion of religious freedom, it will be sufficient rapidly to recall four basic principles which combine to make government constitutional, scil., limited in its powers.

The first principle is the distinction between the sacred and the secular orders of human life. The whole of man's existence is not absorbed in his temporal and terrestrial existence. He also exists for a transcendent end. The power of government does not reach into this higher sacred order of human existence. It has no share in the *cura animarum* or in the *regimen animorum;*[11] it is not the judge or the representative of transcendent truth with regard to man's eternal destiny; it is not man's guide to heaven. Its powers are limited to the affairs of the temporal and terrestrial order of man's existence. And they are not to be used as instruments for the spiritual purposes of the Church —the maintenance of her unity or the furtherance of her mission.

The second principle is the distinction between society and state. Historically, this distinction developed out of the medieval distinction between the *ecclesia (christianitas)* and the *imperium*. The imperial power played a role within Christendom—a limited

[28]

role; it was charged with limited functions within the Great Society inasmuch as the *ecclesia* was a socio-temporal reality. Today, in the developed constitutional tradition, the state is an agency that plays a role within society—a limited role. The purposes of the state are not coextensive with the purposes of society. The state is only one order within society—the order of public law and political administration. The public powers, which are invested with the power of the state, are charged with the performance of certain limited functions for the benefit of society—such functions as can and must be performed by the coercive discipline of law and political power. These functions are defined by constitutional law, in accord with the consent of the people. In general, "society" signifies an area of freedom, personal and corporate, whereas "state" signifies the area in which the public powers may legitimately apply their coercive powers. To deny the distinction is to espouse the notion of government as totalitarian.

The third principle is the distinction between the common good and public order. It follows from the distinction between society and state. The common good includes all the social goods, spiritual and moral as well as material, which man pursues here on earth in accord with the demands of his personal and social nature. The pursuit of the common good devolves upon society as a whole, on all its members and on all its institutions, in accord with the principles of subsidiarity, legal justice, and distributive justice. Public order, whose care devolves upon the state, is a narrower concept. It includes three goods which can and should be achieved by the power which is proper to the state—the power inherent in the coercive discipline of public law. The first is the public peace, which is the highest political good. The second is public morality, as determined by moral standards commonly accepted among the people. The third is justice, which secures for the people what is due to them. And the first thing that is due to the people, in justice, is their freedom, the due enjoyment of their personal and social rights— those empowerments and immunities to which the people, individually, collectively, and corporatively, lay rightful claim. John of Salisbury spoke for the tradition of constitutionalism when he said: "The prince [the constitutional monarch, in contrast to the tyrant] fights for the laws and for the freedom of the people." [12] The power of the state is therefore limited to the maintenance of public order in this threefold sense. (We omit here, as not relevant to our subject, the function of the state with regard to the good of "prosperity," the material welfare of the people.)

The foregoing three principles belong to the order of political truth. When government is based on them, it is based on the truth. The fourth principle is at once a substantive political truth and also the primary rule of political procedure. It is the principle and rule of "freedom under law." The freedom of the people is a political end, prescribed by the personal consciousness among the people. The freedom of the people is also the higher purpose of the juridical order, which is not an end in itself. Furthermore, freedom is the political method *per excellentiam,* prescribed by the political consciousness among the people. In so far as a political society must depend on force and fear to achieve its ends, it departs both from political truth and from the true method of politics. Finally, freedom under law is the basic rule of jurisprudence, which runs thus: "Let there be as much freedom, personal and social, as is possible; let there be only as much restraint and constraint, personal and social, as may be necessary for the public order." In all these ways, the principle and rule of freedom under law sets limits to the power of government.

The Question of Judgment

In reply to this question, the Second View affirms the validity of religious freedom, in the sense explained, as a legal institution, a juridical notion, a civil and human right. Correlatively, it affirms the validity of constitutional government, within whose structure religious freedom, in the sense explained, finds its necessary place. Two things about this compound affirmation must be noted.

First, the Second View undertakes to justify religious freedom, not to idealize it. It is not a question of affirming an ideal instance of constitutional law, after the manner of the First View. The Second View maintains that an ideal instance of constitutional law is a contradiction in terms. In the Second View, therefore, religious freedom is not thesis; neither is it hypothesis. The Second View abandons these categories of systematization. It does not accept, as its basic systematic notion, the abstract notion of the exclusive rights of truth, which creates the disjunction, thesis and hypothesis. Instead, it posits, as the basis for a systematic

[31]

doctrine of religious freedom, the concrete exigences of the personal and political consciousness of contemporary man—his demand for religious freedom, personal and corporate, under a limited government. This demand is approved by reason; it ought to be approved by the authority of the Church. Hence the Second View affirms the validity of an order of constitutional law in which public care of religion is limited to public care of religious freedom in the complex sense already described.

In negative terms, the Second View rejects the opinion that public care of religion necessarily means, per se and in principle, a political and legal care for the exclusive rights of truth and a consequent care to exterminate religious error. In positive terms, it holds that public care of religion is provided in both necessary and sufficient measure when the order of constitutional law recognizes, guarantees, and protects the freedom of the Church, both as a religious community and as a spiritual authority, at the same time that it gives similar recognition, guarantee, and protection to the general religious freedom—personal, ecclesial, associational, and practical—of the whole body politic. Within the new perspectives of today, the Church does not demand, per se and in principle, a status of legal privilege for herself. The Church demands, in principle and in all situations, religious freedom for herself and religious freedom for all men.

Second, the Second View makes its affirmation of religious freedom in full awareness that this affirmation is at once new and traditional. It represents a growth in the understanding of the tradition, which corre-

sponds to the growth of the personal and political consciousness of men today, to the enlargement of the
pastoral solicitude of the Church today, and to the
self-understanding of the Church in the world of today,
as the missionary Church, in the diaspora, the sign of
truth, justice, love, and freedom lifted among the
nations. Therefore the Second View speaks to the
ancient constitutional question of public care of religion in a new historical state of the question. The
answer must be new, because the question is new.
The answer must also be traditional, because it is the
answer of the Church. However, only the elements of
the answer are to be found in the tradition, not the
answer itself in explicit and systematized form.

There are therefore two tasks: (1) to present the
arguments for the affirmation of religious freedom; (2)
to review the tradition, within the new perspectives of
today, in order to show that the affirmation represents
a valid growth in the understanding of the tradition.
Since the concept of religious freedom is complex, the
argument for affirming its validity must be made part
by part. Moreover, since the juridical notion has a
political correlate, the political and juridical arguments will be adduced co-ordinately with the theological and ethical arguments. All the arguments will be
summarily indicated, not fully developed.

Freedom of conscience.—The theological argument
is the tradition with regard to the necessary freedom
of the act of faith which runs unbrokenly from the text
of the New Testament to the Code of Canon Law (can.
1351). This tenet of Catholic doctrine is held no less
firmly by all who bear the name of Christian. In fact,

even the atheist holds it. It is part of the human patrimony of truth, embedded in the common consciousness of mankind. The ethical argument is the immunity of conscience from coercion in its internal religious
decisions. Even the Church, which has authority to
oblige conscience, has no power to coerce it. The political argument is the common conviction that the personal internal forum is immune from invasion by any
powers resident in society and state. No external force
may coerce the conscience of man to any form of belief
or unbelief. The juridical argument enforces the same
conclusion; it is contrary to the nature of civil law to
compel assent to any manner of religious truth or ideology. The distinction between the sacred and the secular is binding on law and government; and the personal
conscience is a sacred forum. Moreover, for the argument here, it does not matter whether the conscience
be true or erroneous. It is not within the competence
of society or state to judge whether conscience be true
or erroneous. And jurisprudence declares the distinction to be irrelevant for the purposes of civil law.

The free exercise of religion.—This, as we have
seen, has three component elements.

Ecclesial or corporate freedom.—The theological
principle here is "the freedom of the Church," the
doctrine celebrated by Gregory VII and restored to its
centrality by Leo XIII. The pregnant phrase expresses
the whole supernatural reality of the Church, as the
community of the faithful and as a spiritual authority
sui iuris. It expresses her distinction from civil society
in origin, constitution, and purposes; it likewise expresses her transcendence to all political forms. In the

[34]

present connection, the phrase asserts the internal autonomy of the Church in the face of the public powers —her right to define her own statute of existence on the basis of the divine will, to determine her own form of organization and government and her own norms of ecclesial life and action, to elect or appoint her own rulers, to educate her own clergy, and to communicate across national boundaries. In all her internal affairs the Church is immune from interference by the public powers. This same claim to internal autonomy is likewise made by other Christian churches, which today reject all forms of Erastianism. Political and legal philosophy acknowledges this ecclesial freedom. The powers of the state are limited to the purposes and interests of the body politic; civil law can deal only with civil affairs. Internal ecclesiastical affairs are no more the concern of the public powers than the affairs of the internal forum of conscience.

Corporate religious freedom also includes the religious freedom of the family and the freedom of the religious school. The Napoleonic concept of *l'état enseignant* and the consequent doctrine of the monopoly of education by the state are contrary to the tradition of constitutionalism and its distinction between society and state.

Freedom of religious association.—First, freedom of affiliation with a religious community is inseparable from personal freedom of conscience. And it is supported by the same arguments. A man's religious affiliation or nonaffiliation is no more the concern of the state than his internal religious decision to believe or not to believe. In both respects he enjoys the same immunity from coercion. The political axiom *Cuius regio, eius et religio,* whereby religious freedom became the prerogative only of the prince, not of the people, is now recognized to be incompatible with both Christian and political principle. Second, freedom of association for religious or charitable purposes derives, on the one hand, from freedom of conscience, and on the other hand, from the general right of voluntary association. This latter right is based on the social nature of man, whose sociality is not exhausted by his citizenship in a body politic. It is likewise based on the principle of subsidiary function as a principle of social organization. The Jacobin revolutionary principle, which abolished all social institutions intermediate between the individual citizen and the state, was a violation of the constitutional tradition.

Freedom of religious expression.—This, as we have seen, is the free exercise of religion in the most formal sense. It is both a personal and also an ecclesial freedom, whose exercise is public, within society, chiefly in the forms of worship, witness, and the teaching of religious doctrine in itself and in its implications for society and state. The argument here is the indissolubility of the link, first, between the internal freedom of the Church and her external freedom to fulfil her apostolic office, and second, between personal freedom of conscience and social freedom of religious expression. The indissolubility of this link is established by a convergence of arguments.

First, the Church, as a community and as an authority, is immune from coercion by the public powers in the discharge of her religious mission, which looks both to the salvation of souls and also, by way of overflow (in the classic Augustinian doctrine), to the creation here on earth of conditions of peace and justice among men and nations. The nineteenth-century rationalist-individualist theory, which would confine the Church "to the sacristy" (in the famous phrase), is incompatible both with the theological doctrine of the freedom of the Church and also with the traditional principles of constitutionalism. These latter confer no power on the state to inhibit the free and public exercise of the Church's mission, much less to define what the mission of the Church is. The French Law of Separation of 1905, for instance, was a flagrant violation of sound political and legal principles. It was a sign, among others, of the final corruption of the constitutional tradition in Europe, which had begun with the rise of absolutism and its twin doctrines of the indivisibility of sovereignty and the complete identity of society and state.

Second, within the complex juridical notion of religious freedom, external freedom of religious expression is inseparably linked with internal freedom of conscience. Lest there be misunderstanding, the exact structure of the argument is to be noted.

The argument does not assert that freedom of religious expression is a logical deduction from freedom of conscience. This manner of argument would imply a hidden premise which is false, namely, a rationalist-individualist conception of man, as if the human person were somehow first an individual and only in the second instance a social being, in such wise that a logical inference could be drawn from individual rights to social rights. Second, the argument makes no appeal to any theory about the rights of the erroneous conscience, whatever may be the value of such a theory. The Second View does not base the juridical notion of freedom of religious expression on such a theory, for the reason already stated, namely, that the truth or error of conscience is not relevant to the constitutional question of public care of religion. Finally, the argument here does not raise the issue of tolerance. Tolerance is a concept of the moral order. It implies a moral judgment on error and the consequent adoption of a moral attitude, based on charity, toward the good faith of those who err. Our present discussion, however, has nothing to do with moral attitudes; it concerns freedom of religious expression as an integral part of the larger juridical notion of religious freedom.

Two lines of argument converge to establish the relation between freedom of conscience and freedom of religious expression. First, a true metaphysic of the human person affirms that human existence is essentially social-historical existence. It is not permitted to introduce a dichotomy into man, to separate his personal-interior existence and his social-historical existence. Hence it is not permitted to recognize freedom of conscience and to deny freedom of religious expression. Both freedoms are given in the same one instance; they are coequal and coordinate, inseparable, equally constitutive of the dignity and integrity of man. A dichotomy between them would rest on a false metaphysic of the human person. From the moral point of view, the dichotomy would be a sort of Kantianism, a separation of the personal-moral and the social-juridical orders. From the political point of view, it would introduce a schism in the body politic, an inequitable classification of citizenship on the basis of religious belief.

The political-legal argument reaches and enforces the same conclusion. In the constitutional tradition, no public official is empowered, by virtue of his public office, to inquire into the theological credentials of any religious body, and to decide whether it exists *iure divino*, whether its doctrine and polity are in conformity with divine revelation, whether it is divinely authorized to conduct public worship, give public witness to its faith, and teach those who are willing to listen. It is not within the competence of the public powers to consign churches to the sacristy, or to exterminate religious opinions from the public domain. The Erastian doctrine that the public powers are the arbiter of religious truth and the architect of church polity is not only contrary to Christian doctrine but also contrary to political principle. Civil law, which has no power to coerce the religious conscience, has no power to coerce the social expressions of the religious conscience. To bring force to bear, in restraint of freedom of religious expression, is to bring force to bear on conscience itself, in restraint of its freedom.

This argument, which is based on metaphysical, ethical, and political principle, is re-enforced by a historical argument. As a matter of historical fact, coercion or constraint of religious worship, witness, or teaching has inevitably resulted in the destruction or diminution of freedom of conscience, from the days of Diocletian to our own day of more subtle and damaging pressures on conscience.

[39]

The limits of the free exercise of religion.—Here is the crucial question. From a practical point of view, society must have some way of protecting itself and its members against abuses committed in the name of the free exercise of religion. And it is the function of the state to provide this protection. From a more theoretical point of view, the free exercise of religion, like the exercise of other cognate civil rights, takes place in the public domain. It is therefore somehow amenable to regulation by the powers which preside over the public domain. Therefore we confront again the crucial issue in the constitutional question of public care of religion. What is the competence of the public powers with regard to passing judgment on forms of religious expression in society? Whence does this competence derive? What are the norms which should govern the action of the public powers in imposing limits, in particular cases, on freedom of religious expression?

The question has had a long history, as we shall indicate. And its history is not yet ended. The Second View maintains that the question admits no ideal solution, that it cannot be settled a priori, *more geometrico,* down to the last detail. It is, however, possible to state certain principles of solution.

First, the care of religion, in so far as it implies the care of souls, is not in any sense a function either of civil society or of the state. Second, the care of religion, in so far as religion is an integral element of the common good of society, devolves upon those institutions whose purposes are religious—the Church and the churches, and various voluntary associations for religious purposes. The school too, in its own way, can

[40]

make a contribution to the religious element in the common good. Third, the care of religion, in so far as it is a duty incumbent on the state, is limited to a care for the religious freedom of the body politic.

It is not exact to say flatly that the state is incompetent in religious matters, as if this were some sort of transtemporal principle, derivative from some eternal law. The exact formula is that the state, under today's conditions of growth in the personal and political consciousness, is competent to do only one thing in respect of religion, that is, to recognize, guarantee, protect, and promote the religious freedom of the people. This is the full extent of the competence of the contemporary constitutional state. From another point of view, constitutional law has done all that is necessary and all that is permissible, when it vindicates to the people what is due to them in justice, namely, their religious freedom. That religious freedom is due to the people in justice is precisely what the personal and political consciousness of contemporary man affirms. Thus it is possible to define, in principle, the functions of constitutional law in our day of the written constitution.

First, freedom of conscience, freedom of religious association, and ecclesial freedom (in the sense of internal autonomy) are to be recognized as absolutely intangible by all legal or extralegal forces. (Obviously, when corporate religious bodies or voluntary associations perform civil acts, such as ownership of property, making contracts, etc., they are subject in these acts to the reasonable regulations of civil law.) Second, personal and corporate freedom of religious expression in worship, witness, teaching, and practice is likewise to be recognized, as inherently related to freedom of conscience and to internal ecclesial freedom. This freedom of religious expression, however, is not absolutely intangible, for the reasons given. Therefore the question arises, what is the criterion which makes limitation of this freedom legitimate.

First, the criterion cannot be theological, scil., the objective theological truth or error involved in some form of public worship, witness, teaching, observance, and practice. The public powers are not competent to make theological judgments. Nor may their action be instrumental in the public enforcement of theological judgments made by the Church. Second, the criterion cannot be ethical, scil., the rightness or wrongness of the personal or collective conscience that prompts particular forms of religious expression. The public powers are not competent to inquire into the norms whereby conscience is formed and to judge their truth or falsity. Third, the criterion is not social, scil., the common good of society. In the first place, the public powers are not the sole judge of what is or is not for the common good. This is a social judgment, to be made by the people, either through a constitutional consent (*consensu iuris*) or through the channels of public opinion. In the second place, in consequence of the distinction between society and state, not every element of the common good is instantly committed to the state to be protected and promoted. Under today's conditions of growth in the personal and political consciousness, this is particularly true of the spiritual goods of the human person, primary among which is religion. Therefore, fourth, the criterion can only be juridical, scil., the exigences of public order in its threefold aspect—political, moral, and juridical.

This is the criterion which governs the action of law and the power of the state in regulating or limiting the exercise of the general civil rights of the citizenry, with which freedom of religious expression is cognate. Hence the public powers are authorized to intervene and to inhibit forms of religious expression (in public rites, teaching, observance, or behavior), only when such forms of public expression seriously violate either the public peace or commonly accepted standards of public morality, or the rights of other citizens. The public powers are competent to make judgments only with regard to the essential exigences of the public order and with regard to the necessity of legal or police intervention in order to protect the public order.

Evidently, this juridical criterion is quite general in its manner of statement. The practical problem lies in its application in given cases. And the casuistry is endless. What chiefly matters is that the application should never be arbitrary. In what concerns religious freedom, the requirement is fourfold: that the violation of the public order be really serious; that legal or police intervention be really necessary; that regard be had for the privileged character of religious freedom, which is not simply to be equated with other civil rights; that the rule of jurisprudence of the free society be strictly observed, scil., as much freedom as possible, as much coercion as necessary.

For the rest, the issues of casuistry, as they arise, will call for a continual dialogue between the public powers and the personal and political consciousness of the citizenry, with a view to finding equitable solutions. In the end, the value of civil law in matters of religion is severely limited. What chiefly matters is that the free exercise of religion should always be responsible—before God, before the rights of others, before the community and its legitimate sensibilities, before the state and its necessary empowerment to effect harmony of rights in cases of conflict. What further matters is the spirit of tolerance, as a moral attitude, among the citizenry—a spirit of reverence and respect for others, which issues in an abhorrence of coercion in religious matters.

One problem in casuistry requires special mention. It centers on the notion of proselytism. In ecumenical thought today a distinction is made between evangelism and proselytism, between responsible evangelical witness or teaching and an irresponsible caricature thereof. The former is regarded as a legitimate exercise of religious freedom; the latter is regarded as the corruption of religious freedom into license. It is, however, difficult to draw the line sharply between these two forms of religious expression (just as it is difficult to draw the line between the legitimate influence of the Church in the temporal order and illegitimate interference of the Church in political affairs). At that, certain characteristics of proselytism can be discerned: the self-assertive aggressiveness that always characterizes propaganda; purely destructive attacks on religious beliefs, institutions, and devotional practices; language or action offensive to the religious sensibilities of the community; the employment of means of seduction, by appeal, for example, to materialist motives; perhaps in particular, efforts to undermine religious faith in the young.

Proselytism is recognized by its style, which is infra-evangelical, unsuited to the gospel of love, contrary to the manner of God's own approach to man, which is full of respect. Proselytism does not stand at the door and knock; it rushes rudely into the house. It is hardly possible to formulate a legal definition of proselytism; it is even less possible to cope with it by the rough instrument of law. Historically, for instance, the problem of the Anabaptists was never equitably solved. Proselytism creates a dilemma for the Christian and political conscience. At bottom, it represents an unchristian use of force in religious matters. Shall it therefore be met by force? The Christian would prefer to show forbearance.

⋆ 2 ⋆

The Tradition

The history of public care of religion as a theological, ethical, political, legal, and jurisprudential problem has been lengthy and involved. Only the most meager outline of it is possible here, sketched chiefly with a view to indicating the changes in the state of the question that have taken place.

The beginnings of the argument go back to the pagan Roman Empire, in which the citizen was permitted his freedom of conscience but compelled to offer sacrifice to the Emperor. The argument assumed Christian form with St. Augustine. He always held firmly to freedom of conscience, the necessary freedom of the Christian act of faith. Nevertheless, he consented to the use of the imperial power to take coercive care of the Donatists. No one today, however, argues the question in his terms, scil., the pragmatic religious value of "salutary constraint," imposed by the public power, as a means for assisting the return of the heretic to the Church. This is not the state of the question today, even in the First View.

The medieval argument was more complicated. The great Hildebrand declared the state of the question in the pregnant phrase that is forever connected with his name, "libertas ecclesiae." Imperial care of religion (the phrase was not medieval but the thing itself was) was limited by the principle of the freedom of the Church, that is, the freedom of the Roman Pontiff and the freedom of the Christian people. The first imperial care of religion was to be a care for the freedom of the Church, a respect for the immunity of the Church from imperial intervention in her internal affairs and in her apostolic office. The essential question was obscured in the Later Middle Ages, when the Gregorian principle of the freedom of the Roman Pontiff was expanded by canonists to the dimensions of the papal prerogative as finally formulated in the doctrine of the two swords and in the system, for instance, of Giles of Rome. The Gregorian state of the question, however, has been restored to full actuality in our present day; it has also been amplified and adapted in the light of new historical circumstances. The question today, as we have seen, is whether public care of religion is not only limited *by* a necessary care for the freedom of the Church, but also limited *to* a care for the freedom of the Church together with a care for the religious freedom of all peoples and all men.

The other pertinent medieval argument dealt with the question, who is to enjoy the "freedom of the Christian people" (*libertas populi christiani*). The argument was made in terms of a distinction between Jews, pagans, and heretics, and it yielded different conclusions. Care of religion meant limited freedom for the Jew, tolerance for the pagan, intolerance for the heretic. The ultimate premise of the argument was concrete and historical, namely, the principle that in the Christian commonwealth the Christian faith was the basis of citizenship, the foundation of all *droit de cité,* the title to the freedom of the Christian people. From this principle the juridical axiom followed, "Extra ecclesiam nullum ius." The axiom did not state an abstract ethical theory (error has no rights); its sense was concrete, historical, constitutional. No one today argues the constitutional question in these terms. The medieval state of the question is archaistic. (A third great medieval argument, about the relation between conscience and the truth, need not detain us here.)

In the post-Reformation era the constitutional question became not only complicated but highly confused. The basic Hildebrandine principle was lost from view. The care of religion by the prince, Catholic or Protestant, came to be determined by the territorial principle (first enunciated by Luther) and by the view, common to Catholics and Protestants (as an afterimage of the medieval doctrine of the two swords), that the power of the prince is to further the cause of religious truth (either Catholic or Protestant, as the case might be) and to persecute error. Gradually, however, the principle of freedom of conscience came to be commonly accepted: "Nec est quisquam puniendus propter conscientiam." But the principle of the free exercise of religion was not accepted. The question therefore arose, what modes of coercion and constraint were or were not incompatible with freedom of conscience. What did the function of public care of religion empower the prince to do with regard to the suppression of public expressions of erroneous religious faith, Catholic or Protestant, as the case might be?

[49]

At first, the dichotomy between freedom of conscience and the free exercise of religion was maintained. Gradually, however, the conviction began to penetrate the common consciousness, Catholic and Protestant, that the link between the two freedoms was more intimate than had been supposed in that individualistic age. Men began to feel that freedom of conscience became meaningless when its public expressions were inhibited. They also began to see that, when outward religious conformity was enforced, freedom of conscience itself was damaged or lost.[13] This growing conviction did not support any concept of religious freedom, but it did enlarge the scope of tolerance.

The conviction seems to have been largely a matter of common sense. In this respect it resembled the gradual recognition of the principle of reciprocity, so called, the political adaptation of the golden rule to the controversy between Catholic and Protestant. At that, common sense is not a bad guide in matters of politics and law. And the fact was that the political and legal aspects of the constitutional question of public care of religion, rather than its theological and ethical aspects, were causing the trouble, in consequence of the unprecedented confusions of the time. Never was there a more disastrous blurring of the classic distinctions made by the constitutional tradition—between the sacred and the secular, between society and state, between the common good and public order. As for the classic rule of jurisprudence, it was stood on its head, to read, "As much coercion as possible; as much freedom as necessary."

In particular, three conceptions of political sovereignty prevailed, which forbade an equitable solution of the constitutional question as a political and juridical question. First, the nation or principality was conceived on the analogy of the family, and the prince was conceived to be *pater patriae,* whose paternal power extended to a care for the total welfare of his subject-children, including their religious welfare. Second, the prince was conceived to be *praecipuum membrum ecclesiae,* whose power was somehow ecclesial in that it extended to a care for the religious unity of his subjects, which was generally considered to be essential to their political unity. Third, the false principle of the indivisibility of sovereignty had become established, and in consequence the religious prerogative of the prince was considered to be simply an essential attribute of his political sovereignty. Care of religion was not the prince's duty; it was his inherent right. And the scope of its exercise was left to his own arbitrary determination. The constitutional question was hopelessly bogged down in this political and juridical morass.

The state of the constitutional question was altered by the ratification of the American Constitution (1789) and its Bill of Rights (1791). The question ceased to be asked in terms of political and legal support of the exclusive rights of truth, with consequent intolerance of error. The question was asked, and answered, in terms of religious freedom—personal, ecclesial, associational, practical. The premise of the answer was the restoration, in a new form adapted to new circumstances, of ancient and medieval constitutionalism. Religious freedom as a legal institution, which was formally created by the First Amendment, stood in harmonious relation

[51]

with the political conception of government as limited in its powers, which was stated in the Constitution. Public care of religion by the state became legal care of "the free exercise of religion" in society. By establishing a form of government and an order of constitutional law that were both new and also a renewal of traditional principles, the people of the United States altered the state of the historic constitutional question of public care of religion. The alteration was effected by a consensual act of the people; this in itself was a singular historical event.

At the time, no *raison d'église* obliged the Church to reckon with the new development. There were less than 30,000 Catholics in the new Federal Republic. Moreover, the Church was immediately plunged into the lengthy and bitter conflict with the French Revolution. Prominently at issue in the conflict was a concept of religious freedom that was totally different—in its premises, meaning, import, and purport—from the concept embodied in the First Amendment to the American Constitution. No one, then or later, took official notice of the difference. The attention of the Church, from Pius VI to Pius IX, was totally engaged in the condemnation and containment of the new European revolutionary ideology.

The next constructive phase of the constitutional question was inaugurated by Leo XIII. He read the signs of the times, as every Pope does. Two were decisive for the orientation of his doctrinal instruction and pastoral solicitude. They were visible in the traditionally Catholic nations of Europe. The first was the phenomenon of the "illiterate masses" (*imperita multi-*

tudo), which was basic to the doctrine of *Libertas,* as the same phenomenon in the form of the "people in misery" (*miserum vulgus*) was basic to the doctrine of *Rerum novarum.* The statistics of illiteracy at the time are well known. The masses were also religiously untutored, politically inert, economically powerless, deficient in both the personal and political consciousness. The second sign of the times was the spread of totalitarian democracy (as it is called today), both as a quasi-religious ideology and also as a political regime, whose purpose was to effect the apostasy of the masses, the destruction of traditional Catholic culture, the establishment of a new morality, a new politics, a new historical-social order.

The basic philosophical tenet was the theory of the "outlaw conscience" (*conscientia exlex*), the absolute autonomy of the individual human reason.[14] The political transcription of this basic tenet of rationalism was the theory of the juridical omnipotence and omnicompetence of the state.[15] Implicit in the theory was the unity and indivisibility of the national sovereignty. Consequent on the theory was the obliteration of all distinction between society and state. The whole of social life was subsumed under the power of the totalitarian state.

The state conceived its religious prerogative in terms of its own omnicompetence. Like the autonomous individual reason of which it was the political embodiment, it became the supreme arbiter of religious truth and church polity. Its theological judgment, based on the rationalist principle, was that all religions are equally true as equal expressions of the individual outlaw conscience. On the basis of this judgment, the state promulgated the *ius commune*, the statute of religious freedom. All religions are to be equal in their rights within society, because they are all equal in their inherent truth. The *ius commune* was an act of omnipotent sovereignty, which positively authorized the existence of all religions within the society-state on an equality of legal footing which corresponded to their equality in theological truth. Moreover, the indivisibility of sovereignty permitted no other public authority to exist in society. Hence the Church and the churches were assigned the equal statute of purely voluntary associations, whose right to existence and action derived solely from the juridically omnicompetent state. Thus the Church was incorporated into the juridical order of the state and made subject to the "unlimited and lawless government" (*principatus sine modo sine lege*), in Leo's phrase, of rationalist political theory. In technical law, the Church had no public existence. Public religion was a *contradictio in adiecto*. Officially, the state—that is, the whole of public life—was atheist. Religion was a purely private affair.

This was the conception of religious freedom as a legal institution, and the corresponding conception of the state as a totalitarian power, that confronted Leo XIII. Like his predecessors, but on the basis of a far more acute analysis of historical and political reality, he condemned both the legal institution and the ideology that inspired it. It was not possible then to make a distinction between the institution and the ideology. The institution was vicious in its principle; it was condemned in itself and in its principle.

What Leo XIII confronted was the post-Reformation confessional nation-state *à rebours*. It was the lineal progenitor of the people's democracy of contemporary Communist theory. The public philosophy was atheism; it alone had public rights. Religion had no public rights; it was to be exterminated from the public domain by the power of the state. This juridical order and this form of polity were characterized in rationalist theory as "ideal." To the rationalist mentality, which is untouched by historical consciousness, discourse about "ideals" in law and politics is congenial. The rationalist deals in theses, in ideological propositions that are not derived from historical reality but are to be imposed upon it.

Leo XIII was not untouched by the logic of contradiction; no controversialist ever is. Hence he constructed his own conception of the confessional state. He made his defense of the *status quo ante*. In common with the whole European Church in the nineteenth century, he formed part of what is called the Conservative Reaction. (Today, when we have come to understand better the price of revolution, this movement receives more kindly judgment at the hands of historians.) Five aspects of the Leonine theory of the confessional state require comment.

First, he adopted the theory of the ethical society-state (*Kulturstaat*), proper to the postmedieval era, whose roots are in Plato. It is difficult to find in Leo XIII the classic distinction between society and state (except in *Rerum novarum*). The distinction had been lost from view during the absolutist era. Correlatively, nowhere in some eighty-eight documents that deal with political or religio-political affairs did Leo XIII ever develop a complete philosophy of law and jurisprudence, in the style of St. Thomas' treatise *De lege*. He was a moralist, not a lawyer. As portrayed in his text, the society-state had the four classic characteristics. It was built upon a conception of the common good. The total care of the common good was committed to the *principes* (Leo's favorite word); hence the disappearance of the distinction between society and state. The social order was to be constructed from the top down, by the action of the rulers. The citizen appears simply as subject, whose single duty is obedience to rule. The cachet of the theory is in the maxim that Leo quotes: "Qualis rex, talis grex." This theory met the needs of the time, specified by the phenomenon of the illiterate, inert masses.

Second, against the lawless and unlimited government of rationalist theory, Leo XIII developed the true notion of political authority, derivative from God, subject in its uses to the divine law, directed in its action to the common good. In his own idiom and for his own day he wrote a *Speculum principis christiani*. In this great *aggiornamento* of the medieval *Fürstenspiegel,* the ruler appears as the servant of God, the architect of the social order, the supreme agent responsible for the Christian quality of social life.

Third, Leo XIII accepted the analogy, common in post-Reformation theory, between civil society and domestic society. The ruler appears in *Libertas* as paterfamilias, who is "to govern in kindly fashion and with a sort of fatherly love." [16] In *Immortale Dei* the subjects appear as children, who are "to be obedient to

[56]

their rulers and show them reverence and loyalty, with a certain species of that *pietas* which children show their parents." [17] In this paternal conception of rule, the power of the ruler extends to a care for the total welfare of his children-subjects, the illiterate masses. His *patria potestas* is to protect them, since they cannot protect themselves, in their possession of the patrimony of Christian truth that has been their heritage in the traditionally Catholic nation. To this end the ruler is to repress the "offenses of the unbridled mind," which are like "injuries violently wrought upon the weak." [18]

Fourth, Leo XIII accepted an adaptation of the territorial principle of the post-Reformation era, the principle that in one "city" (*civitas*) only one faith should be publicly professed.[19] This, incidentally, is not the dogma of faith that all men are called by God through Christ to unity of religious faith in the one Church. The dogma states a thesis whose realization is to be eschatological. Leo XIII "temporalized" the thesis; his premise was historical—the traditional unity of faith in the Catholic nations of Europe. In the one "city" the one public faith should obviously be the true faith, certainly in those "cities" which have been traditionally Catholic. The Catholic faith ought to enjoy the favor of the law and the protection of the ruler, as part of his paternal care for the common good and for the total welfare, including the religious welfare, of his subject-children. Certainly, little support of the Church could be expected from the illiterate masses; it was they who needed the protection of the ruler. With complete realism, Leo XIII saw that the reliance of the Church had to be on the heads of state.

Fifth, Leo XIII permitted the ruler to tolerate the legal institution of religious freedom, in given circumstances, for the sake of gaining or guarding some greater good or for the sake of avoiding some greater evil. Nothing more than tolerance could be granted to the institution in the only historical sense in which Leo XIII understood it—the sense given to the institution by Continental sectarian Liberalism. In this sense, the institution was not a legitimate exigence of the personal and political consciousness, which at the time did not exist in the illiterate masses. It was an outrageous act of totalitarian sovereignty, based on a rationalist ideology that was, in effect, the destruction of human dignity.

Thus Leo XIII brought to its final term of development the theory of the confessional state. Nothing has been added to it since his day, except perhaps its qualification as the "ideal instance" of constitutional law. Leo XIII never uses the word "ideal." What impresses the student of his doctrine is not any quality of idealism, but a strong sense of historical realism. As the whole tenor of his pontificate shows, Leo XIII was not lacking in the historical consciousness.

In another respect, Leo XIII laid the foundations for a new development of doctrine, a new growth in the understanding of the Christian tradition which Vatican Council I laid as an enduring imperative on the Church.[20] The Leonine development was accomplished, as all legitimate development must be accomplished, by a *ressourcement,* a creative return to the sources of the tradition, a review of traditional doctrine within a new perspective created by history. The

Leonine perspective was created by the fact that totalitarian democracy, in the style of Continental sectarian Liberalism, had renewed in a more vicious form than ever the confusion of the sacred and the secular orders of human life which had been the disastrous legacy of the post-Reformation era. Hence Leo XIII recalls the tradition of the dyarchy, which is the first principle in Christian constitutionalism.

Moreover, he states the doctrine in a developed form of understanding that was unprecedented, a new thing in papal utterances. The dyarchy is not left in its medieval form of understanding—the doctrine of the two powers in the one Great Society, the *ecclesia*. In Leo's understanding, there are two societies, two orders of law, and two powers. There are seven major texts, which cover his whole pontificate. They are found in *Arcanum* (1880), *Nobilissima Gallorum gens* (1884), *Immortale Dei* (1885), *Officio sanctissimo* (1887), *Sapientiae christianae* (1890), *Praeclara gratulationis* (1894), and *Pervenuti* (1902).

This reiterated statement of the dyarchy, in developed form, is the very heart of Leo's doctrine on constitutionalism. He emphasized in a new way the transcendence of the Church, both as a spiritual authority and as the People of God, who are ruled by His law, revealed in Christ. He also emphasized in a new way the relative autonomy of the secular order of human life—the proper autonomy of the People Temporal, who are ruled by a civil law, under a government whose powers are limited by a higher order of law not of its own making.

Leo XIII did not pursue the consequences of this

latter emphasis. It would have been inappropriate, as well as impossible, to pursue them in a day when the People Temporal were so largely illiterate, culturally and religiously, and consequently incapable of asserting their rightful autonomy, their empowerment to judge, direct, and correct the processes of political rule and legal action. In any case, Leo XIII opened the door to the developments which became visible in Pius XII and John XXIII. For the rest, his statement of the autonomy of the socio-political order dissipated the afterimage of medieval *christianitas,* which for so long had hung more or less heavily over the Catholic nation-states. Thereafter *christianitas* on the medieval model would be archaism. His statement also condemned the confusion of religion and politics that still existed, not least in the Catholic nation-states.[21] Finally, the statement of Leo prepared the way for a change in the state of the question of public care of religion. Implicit in the statement was a declaration of the freedom of the people, once the people had fulfilled the conditions of freedom, which are the growth of the personal and political consciousness. And implicit in the freedom of the people is religious freedom as a juridical institution correlative with constitutional government as a form of polity.

In another respect, the Leonine statement of the dyarchy at once effected a development of doctrine and opened the door to further developments. It restored to its proper centrality the Gregorian doctrine of the freedom of the Church, which had been lost from view in the post-Reformation era.

It would not be consonant with the evidence of the

texts to say that Leo XIII's master idea, in what concerns public care of religion, was the notion of the exclusive rights of truth and the rightlessness of error. He does indeed blast the silly rationalist notion that all ideas are equally true and rightful, because they are all equally free as expressions of the autonomous reason. He insists on the tautology that truth is truth and error is error. He also insists that the criterion of truth and error is not freedom. He further insists that truth and error, right and wrong do not enter the juridical order on an equal title, which was the other rationalist sophism. What is true or right may receive positive juridical authorization; what is false or evil can receive only juridical tolerance. This, incidentally, is the only concrete juridical sense that can possibly attach to the otherwise unhelpful abstraction, that error has no rights. No sensible man would quarrel with this concrete sense. The point at the moment, however, is that this Leonine doctrine, directed against the basic tenet of rationalism, was not his central notion in the question of public care of religion.

His central notion was "the freedom of the Church." One could begin to appreciate its centrality by counting the number of times that the phrase, or an equivalent of it, appears in his writings (some eighty-one times in sixty documents). A more positive proof emerges from a study of the texts on the dyarchy. It is clear that the doctrine of the freedom of the Church is equally as central as the doctrine of the dyarchy itself. Freedom is the first property of the Church; and freedom is the first claim that the Church makes in the face of society and state: "This freedom is so much the property of the Church, as a perfect and divine work, that those who act against this freedom likewise act against God and against their duty." [22]

The decisive proof results from an understanding of the structure of Leo XIII's controversy with Continental sectarian Liberalism, and with its notion of religious freedom as a legal institution that stood in correlation with a form of polity in which government was "lawless and unlimited." The essential vice of the system was not that the liberalist state granted equal rights to truth and error and dethroned the Church from its historic status of legal privilege. The essential vice was that this political and juridical system destroyed the freedom of the Church. Thus it attacked the very nature of the Church as a community, an order of law, and a spiritual authority. The basic line of battle was drawn by Proposition 39 of the *Syllabus*: "The state, inasmuch as it is the origin and source of all rights, possesses a power of jurisdiction that knows no limits."

The texts are numerous and formal. They begin with *Inscrutabili* (1878) and its indictment of what Leo later will call the "new regalism," which "makes [the Church] subservient to the sovereignty of political rulers." [23] So too *Immortale Dei*: "In this kind of political order, presently so much admired, it is a deliberate policy either to drive the Church wholly out of public existence or to hold her bound and fettered to the regime." [24] So again *Libertas* and its protest against the politicization of the Church: "Accordingly, they falsify the nature of this divine society; they diminish and inhibit her authority, her teaching, all her action.

At the same time, they aggrandize the power of civil government to the point of subjecting the Church of God to its sovereign rule, as if the Church were just another voluntary association of citizens." [25] *Et alibi pluries.*

Proposition 39 of the *Syllabus* was the destruction of the freedom of the Church. Hence Leo XIII was led to restore this doctrine to the rightful centrality that it had in the tradition. He was Hildebrand redivivus. The essential care of religion that devolves upon the public powers is not a care for the exclusive rights of truth and for the extermination of error. It is a care for the freedom of the Church. The phrase is pregnant with multiple meanings, which Leo XIII specified. It is not, however, pregnant with the concept of "establishment," the status of legal privilege for the Church, with the consequent status of legal disadvantage for other religious bodies. Leo XIII never draws this conclusion from his central doctrine. He does indeed draw the conclusion, but from other premises of a more historically conditioned kind.

Proposition 39 of the *Syllabus* was also the destruction of the essential dignity of man, which resides in his freedom. Leo XIII did not greatly attend to this aspect of the matter; it did not lie within his historical problematic. However, by his central emphasis on the freedom of the Church he at once reinstated the Gregorian state of the question of public care of religion and thus also opened the way to a widening of the question, thus stated, to include the issue of the freedom of the human person—the issue of religious freedom as a legal institution within a system of constitutional government, correspondent to the legitimate exigences of the personal and political consciousness.

Pius XII, in his turn, read the signs of the times and discerned two that gave direction to his doctrine and pastoral solicitude. The first was totalitarian tyranny on the Communist model. Now the threat was not simply to the freedom of the Church in the traditionally Catholic nations of Europe; the new threat was to the freedom of the people everywhere. An ideology and a system of rule were abroad, "which in the end rejected and denied the rights, the dignity, and the freedom of the human person." [26] The problematic that had been only implicit in Leo XIII's time had now become terribly explicit. The full implications of Proposition 39 of the *Syllabus* had been realized. The second sign of the times was the rise of the personal and political consciousness: "The people have been awakened, as it were, from a lengthy dormancy. In the face of the state and in the face of their rulers they have assumed a new attitude—questioning, critical, distrustful. Taught by bitter experience, they oppose with increasing vehemence the monopolistic reaches of a power that is dictatorial, uncontrollable, and intangible. And they demand a system of government that will be more in accord with the dignity and freedom of the citizenry." [27]

The mission of the Church, therefore, must include the vindication of the "dignity of man." [28] The goal of Pius XII's pontificate, which he recommended as a goal for all men of good will, was "to give back to the human person the dignity with which he was endowed by God from the beginning." [29] To this end, a new social

[64]

order had to be constructed, based on this principle: "The purpose of all social life remains always the same, always sacred and obligatory, namely, the development of the personal values of man as the image of God." [30] Proceeding from these premises, Pius XII made his first contribution to the development of doctrine in the matter of religious freedom. It consisted in his development of the concept of government as constitutional, that is, limited in its powers.

He abandons Leo XIII's ethical concept of the society-state, with its four classic characteristics. Instead he adopts the juridical concept of the state (*Rechtsstaat*), whose genesis owed more to Christian inspiration. The state is only one order of action within society; it is an agent of society for certain limited purposes. Society and state are not built on a generic conception of the common good, but on a concrete conception of the human person in the present historical moment, marked by the rise of the personal and political consciousness. The basic notion in Pius XII's sociopolitical philosophy is thus stated: "Man as such is by no means to be considered the object of social life or a sort of inert element in it; on the contrary, he is the subject, the foundation, and the end of social life." [31] The Pope revalidates the fundamental insight that gave rise to the constitutional tradition, the "free man, bound by duties, endowed with inviolable rights, who is the origin and end of human society." [32]

Therefore the primary function of government is a function with regard to the juridical order: "To protect the inviolable rights that are proper to man, and to have a care that everyone may more readily discharge his duties—this is the chief function of the public power." [33]

Therefore too the function of government with regard to the common good is limited:

Does not this principle [the juridical function of government] bring out the genuine meaning of the common good which the state is called upon to promote? From this principle it follows that the care of the common good does not imply such an extensive power over the members of the community that, in virtue of it, public authority would be allowed to restrict the expansion of individual human action, as described above, or to make direct decisions with regard to the beginning or the termination (except in the case of legitimate punishment) of human life, or to determine on its own cognizance what should be the movement of human life—physical, spiritual, religious, and moral—in such a way as to come in conflict with the personal rights and duties of man. [34]

Here, as elsewhere, Pius XII shows his awareness of the distinction between society and state, between the total common good of society and the elements of the common good that are committed to the power of the state. In his own idiom, the distinction is between the wider order of "social life" and the narrower "juridical order" of society.

Therefore, again, Pius XII abandons completely the Leonine notion of government as paternal. The relationship between ruler and ruled is only political, not familial. The citizen is not a child. Still less is he the mere passive object of rule. He is to be an active participant in the fashioning of his own social and political destiny. In Pius XII's conception, society and state are to be built, as it were, from the bottom up—on the human person and by the human person, or, in more formally political terms, on the consent of the people and by the consent of the people.

Therefore, finally, the nineteenth-century polarity —the illiterate masses and the *principes*—is dissolved. Now the terms of political life are the "true people" (as distinct from the "masses") and the public powers as representative of the people, united with the people in the traditional political effort to achieve an "ideal of freedom and equality." [35]

Thus Pius XII effected a badly needed *aggiornamento* of the official political philosophy of the Church. He relinquished the elements in Leo XIII's philosophy that had become archaistic. He brought the Church abreast of the developments in the constitutional tradition that were demanded by the new personal and political consciousness.

Constitutional government, limited in its powers, dedicated to the defense of the rights of man and to the promotion of the freedom of the people, is the political correlate of religious freedom as a juridical notion, a civil and human right, personal and corporate. By advancing the doctrine of constitutional government, Pius XII moved along the way opened by Leo XIII, towards a change in the state of the question of public care of religion. Moreover, if his doctrine is considered as a whole, in itself and in its tendency, within the perspectives set by his insight into the signs of the times, it may be maintained that he helped to constitute the ancient question in a new state. He took a step beyond Pius XI, who was himself in the Gregorian tradition that had been renewed by Leo XIII.

Pius XI rejected the formula "freedom of con-

science," because to his ears it still bore connotations
of the rationalist theory of the outlaw conscience. However, against the invasions of the Fascist totalitarian
state, he undertook "to fight the good fight for freedom
of consciences." [36] In the context, it would seem, he was
continuing the ancient fight for the freedom of the
Church, as the community of the faithful. This is what
he defended against the operations of Proposition 39 of
the *Syllabus* which were still visible in Mexico: "As a
society of men, the Church has absolute need of a just
freedom of action for the enjoyment and growth of her
own life; and the faithful have the right to live in civil
society according to the dictates of reason and conscience." [87]

Pius XI was in the Gregorian tradition, as Pius XII
would also be: "Wherefore We . . . address all civil
rulers and all those who are in any way in charge of
public affairs, and We solemnly assert that the Church
must always enjoy a due freedom, in order to pursue
her work of education, to impart truth to the mind, to
impress justice on the spirit, and to refresh both mind
and spirit with the divine love of Jesus Christ." [38]
Again, when Pius XII comes to declare the essential
exigences of the Church within society and state, to be
recognized in a concordat, the declaration takes this
form: "Concordats ought therefore to assure to the
Church a stable condition in law and in fact in the
state with which they are concluded, and guarantee the
Church a full independence in the fulfilment of her
divine mission." [39] The formulation is in terms of the
Gregorian-Leonine principle. Nothing is said about a
situation of legal privilege as per se a claim of the

Church. Nor is it implied that only such a legal situation of establishment as the one religion of the state would assure the requisite legal and social stability and freedom of the Church.

Already under Pius XI the problematic of religious freedom began to widen in consequence of the crudities of Nazi totalitarianism and its sweeping attack on all manner of religion, Catholic and Protestant. Therefore Pius XI took the forward step of assuming the patronage of the freedom of all religious men: "The man of religious faith has an inalienable right to profess his faith and to practice it in appropriate ways. Laws which repress or render difficult the profession and practice of religious faith are in contradiction with a law of nature." [40] This statement rests on a general premise, "that man as a person possesses God-given rights which must remain immune from any invasion on the part of society that would deny, annul, or diminish them." [41] The problematic is developing. The freedom of the Church as the community of the faithful is not the sole object of the Church's concern. The freedom of the human person in his belief in God is also to be recognized and protected against unjust encroachments by legal or social forces.

Pius XII accepts this wider problematic of religious freedom. Among the "fundamental rights of the person," which are to be recognized and promoted by the juridical order of society, he includes the "right to private and public worship of God, including also religious action of a charitable kind." [42] Religious freedom as a juridical notion, which required legal recognition and protection, has emerged into clarity. In this juridi-

[69]

cal sense, religious freedom is an integral element in the freedom of the people, which sets limits to the powers of the state. It is a freedom in which all the people equally share, without discrimination on the score of particular forms of religious belief. Moreover, religious freedom in its universal juridical sense is a proper object of legal and social care. In the constitutional order of a society in which the personal and political consciousness is active, public care of religion becomes a care for the religious freedom of the Church and likewise a care for the religious freedom, personal and corporate, of the human person as such.

This affirmation, presently being made by the Second View, is fully in consonance with the doctrine of Pius XII. It is also fully in continuity with the growth in the understanding of the tradition which had been inaugurated by Leo XIII's renewal of the Gelasian and Gregorian tradition. The two essential junctures of ideas have, in effect, been made. The first juncture is between the two correlative exigences of the personal and political consciousness—between constitutional government (Pius XII's juridical state), limited in its powers by a necessary respect for human rights, and the concept of religious freedom as a general civil and human right, claiming the protection of the juridical order of society. The second juncture is between the ancient historic defense of the freedom of the Church and the newly necessary defense of the freedom of the people. In the present moment of history the freedom of the people of God is inseparably linked with the freedom of the peoples of the world. What the pastoral solicitude of the Church today demands, the developed

doctrine of the Church likewise proclaims and authorizes, namely, a universal care for religious freedom in
society and state.

One document of Pius XII requires special attention, the Allocution to the Congress of Italian Catholic
Jurists of December 6, 1953.[43] The document must be
regarded as one of the Pope's occasional deliberate
efforts to fall short of complete lucidity. The purpose
was achieved in the present case; this document has
been cited by both parties to the present controversy,
between the First and the Second Views. In any event,
the major doctrinal intention of the document is plain,
namely, to clarify an issue of jurisprudence with regard
to the legal institution of intolerance. The Pope's
chosen universe of discourse is the problem of public
care of religion as a problem within the international
juridical community presently being formed. Four
propositions immediately emerge with adequate clarity.

First, throughout the document the Pope uses the
vocabulary of "tolerance." However, what he is talking
about is the immunity of the citizen from coercion by
the public powers in his religious profession and practice. This is precisely the definition of religious freedom in its contemporary juridical sense, explained
above. Hence it cannot be maintained that the Pope
refuses to acknowledge the concept of religious freedom. The issue of vocabulary is trivial.

Second, the Pope asserts that the theological question of objective religious truth, and the moral question of the obligations of conscience toward what is
objectively true and good, are not proper matters for
political discussion or legal decision by individual

[71]

states or by the international community. What confronts the statesman or jurist is the constitutional question, namely, the question of the use of legal coercion in religious matters.[44]

Third, the Pope implies that a statute of religious freedom throughout the international community, subject to restriction only by the exigences of the public order, would be acceptable to the Church and ought to be acceptable to the Catholic state. By religious freedom he means the immunity of the citizens from coercion in "the free exercise of their own ethical and religious beliefs and practices, in so far as these do not violate the penal laws of the state in which they dwell." [45]

Fourth, in continuity with all his predecessors the Pope rejects the solution of the constitutional question, and the consequent concept of religious freedom, that were proper to nineteenth-century European sectarian Liberalism. The solution, as we have seen, took the form of an act of sovereignty whereby the state positively authorized the existence and action of religious error and positively conferred upon truth and error an equal social and legal mandate. This solution and this concept of religious freedom, as we have likewise seen, are outlawed not only by Catholic theological and ethical principle but also by the political and legal principles of constitutionalism.

With these simple matters out of the way, the Pope approaches with considerable delicacy his central issue, which is the jurisprudence of legal intolerance. His question is, what is the ultimate and most general rule of jurisprudence in terms of which the legal institution

[72]

of intolerance is to be justified. The question is theoretical, a *quaestio iuris*.

Is it to be maintained that this ultimate rule of
legal action is a duty, per se incumbent on the state,
to repress religious and moral deviations? If this is so,
it follows that such deviations are to be repressed by
the state, whenever and as far as it is possible for the
state to repress them. The state would fail in its duty,
if it were to tolerate religious and moral errors in circumstances in which their repression was possible. Such
tolerance would be immoral.

The Pope denies both the premise and the conclusion of this system of jurisprudence. He denies the
premise: "The duty to repress moral and religious deviations cannot therefore be considered an ultimate
norm of action." [46] He denies the conclusion: "Hence
the affirmation: Religious and moral aberration ought
always to be suppressed, as far as repression is possible,
because tolerance of them is in itself immoral, cannot
be sustained in its unconditioned absoluteness." [47] The
Pope goes on to assert that this rule of jurisprudence
is unknown to the civil and Christian tradition:
"Neither the common conviction of men, nor the
Christian conscience, nor the sources of revelation, nor
the practice of the Church recognize such a rule." [48]
Thus the Pope fulfils his severely limited doctrinal
intention, which was to make clear that the possibility
of legal repression of error and evil is not the juridical
criterion that justifies such repression.

However, he carries his doctrine one step farther.
The rule of jurisprudence, that religious and moral
deviations are always to be repressed by the state, as

far as it is possible to repress them, rested for its validity on an ethical premise: "That which does not correspond with truth and the norm of morality has, objectively, no right either to existence or to dissemination or to action." Here the Pope grants the premise, but still refuses the conclusion. The premise merely asserts the obvious truth that there is an objective distinction between truth and error, good and evil. It also implies that truth and goodness may receive the positive sanction of law, whereas error and evil may not. This too is obvious. The question is whether one may draw from this ethical axiom the jurisprudential conclusion that, whenever the state can repress error and evil, it ought to repress them, as a matter of primary and ultimate duty. The Pope refuses this conclusion. The only legitimate conclusion is that the state may never positively authorize the existence, dissemination, or activity of what is erroneous or evil.

For the rest, the Pope does not deny that the state has a duty to repress religious and moral deviations, or, in broader terms, that care of religion is a duty incumbent on the state. No one who is acquainted with the civil and Christian tradition of constitutionalism will deny this. The question has always been, and still is, what is the rule of jurisprudence which justifies the use of coercive measures in fulfilment of this duty. In more general terms, what is the competence of the state with regard to religious matters? In reply to this positive question, the Pope is content to make three general affirmations.

First, he affirms that the question cannot be decided in the abstract; there is need always to consider the

relativities of history, the diversity of factual circumstances. A priori discourse about duties that per se
devolve upon the state is illegitimate and useless, for
one simple reason: "It can happen that in determinate
circumstances He [God] does not confer upon man
any mandate, does not impose any duty, does not even
give any right to inhibit or repress that which is erroneous and false." [49] The *quaestio iuris,* about the
duties and rights of the state with regard to the care
of religion, is inherently a historical question, not an
abstract one. Every answer to it is necessarily hypothesis, an answer conditioned by circumstances, an application of principles within a determined situation of
fact. The disjunction between thesis and hypothesis
is factitious.

Second, he affirms that, from the standpoint of the
Church, the supreme juridical principle that governs
the constitutional question is the common good of the
Church, both as a national and as an international
entity.[50] From his other writings it is clear that the good
of the Church consists essentially in two things: first,
exact observance of the requirements of the Gelasian-
Leonine dyarchy, and second, full assurance of the freedom of the Church. From the standpoint of the statesman, the juridical criterion for the limitation of
religious freedom is the exigences of public order, as
specified in penal laws.[51]

Third, he affirms the competence of the "jurist"
with regard to the *quaestio facti,* scil., what are the
determinate exigences of the good of the Church and
of the public order of society in given circumstances.
Since the *quaestio facti* is a question of constitutional

law, whose justice must rest on the consent of the governed, the "jurist" here is the citizen, or better, the people as a whole. Finally, the Pope affirms the necessity of a dialogue between the Church and the jurist-people in the process of reaching a mutually satisfactory solution of the *quaestio facti*.

It is not difficult to assemble from the vast corpus of Pius XII all the principles that were marshaled above in support of the Second View: (1) the theological principles—the dyarchy, the freedom of the Church, the freedom of the act of faith; (2) the ethical principles—religious freedom as the rightful exigence of the contemporary personal and political consciousness; the insight that the free man, bound by duties and endowed with rights, is the origin and end of the social order; (3) the political principles—that the public power is not the judge of religious truth or of the secrets of conscience; that the primary function of the public powers is the vindication of the juridical order of human and civil rights, i.e., the fostering of the freedom of the people; (4) the juridical principle—that the criterion for public restriction of religious freedom is some necessary requirement of public order; (5) the jurisprudential principle—that necessity, not possibility, is the further criterion for coercive inhibition of the free exercise of religion.

The principles are all stated, but they are not systematized, and the conclusion to which they point is not explicitly drawn. At that, the basic concept for a work of systematization has gradually emerged, beginning with Leo XIII—the freedom of the Church as allied, in the present historical juncture, with the freedom of the peoples of the world. At the same time, the ancient problem of public care of religion has emerged in a new state of the question.

The state of the question proper to the post-Reformation and Liberalist eras is now archaistic—the care of religion as the care for the exclusive rights of truth and for the consequent extermination of error. There has been a return to the traditional theological state of the question, in its Gregorian form, public care of the freedom of the Church. Today, however, in the new circumstances of our own age, marked by the growth of the personal and political consciousness, the Gregorian state of the question, reinstated by Leo XIII and confirmed by Pius XII in the line of Pius XI, has necessarily been widened. The public care of religion which the doctrine and pastoral solicitude of the Church today require and authorize is care of religious freedom, in the complex sense approved by the common consciousness of men.

This affirmation, to which the Second View concludes after a review of the tradition within the new perspectives created by the historical moment, is strongly confirmed by John XXIII. He situated himself firmly within the Gregorian tradition. Moreover, with the historical consciousness that was his mark, he broadened even more explicitly than Pius XII the problematic of religious freedom in the light of the signs of the times.

Speaking of the work of the coming Council, he voices the primary traditional concern and claim of

[77]

the Church, to which the Council would turn its attention:

> What is to be said about the relations between the Church and civil society? We live in the face of a new political world. One of the fundamental rights which the Church cannot renounce is the right to religious freedom, which is not simply freedom of worship. The Church claims and teaches this freedom, and for the sake of it she continues to suffer grievous penalties in many countries. The Church cannot renounce this freedom, because it is of the essence of the service which she is bound to render. This service is not offered as a corrective or a complement of that which other institutions are required to render or have appropriated to themselves. It is an essential and irreplaceable element of the design of Providence, in order to set men on the way of truth. Truth and freedom are the foundation stones upon which the edifice of human civilization is erected.[52]

The centrality of the Gregorian principle is evident. Moreover, the last sentence adumbrates in advance the theme of *Pacem in terris*.[53] This Encyclical consciously builds on Pius XII and his conception of the juridical state as the servant of the free man and the free society. What concerns us here is that John XXIII makes more explicit the new state of the question of public care of religion and speaks more directly to the question in its new state. It will be sufficient briefly to indicate the two major contributions that he made to the development of Catholic doctrine on the subject.

First, the juncture between the two correlative exigences of the personal and political consciousness is made explicit in the very structure of the Encyclical. The concept of constitutional government is more sharply described than in Pius XII,[54] even to the point of recommending, for the first time in papal documents, the written constitution.[55] And this concept of the limited functions of the state is brought into explicit correlation with a fully developed description of the juridical order of human and civil rights and freedoms, whose protection and promotion is the primary function of the state.[56] This is Pius XII, of course, but speaking with a new accent—more affirmative, more confident that the present moment in history is the term of a progress that has been real, even though not unambiguous.

Moreover, within the juridical order of human and civil rights the right to religious freedom is firmly situated: "This too is to be numbered among the rights of man, that he should be able to worship God in accord with the norm approved by his conscience (*ad rectam conscientiae suae normam*) and to profess his religion privately and publicly."[57] The declaration is not ambiguous, as some have maintained. It is to be understood within the context of the Encyclical and its concept of the juridical state. Obviously, the Pope cannot espouse the theory of *conscientia exlex*; he asserts that conscience must be formed by higher norms (*conscientia recta*). But for the purposes of civil life, in order that conscience may possess the status of personal and civil right in the face of the public power, it is not required that the norms whereby conscience is formed should be true (*conscientia vera*).

The reason is the traditional one, namely, that the public power is not the judge of the truth or falsity of the norms whereby conscience is formed. The public power is obliged to respect the personal or corporate conscience as such, for the precise reason that conscience is subject to higher norms which the public power cannot legislate. To deny this is to affirm Proposition 39 of the *Syllabus, quod absit.* John XXIII touches the tradition in speaking of the mode of action of public authority: "Since all men are equal in their natural dignity, no one has the power to force another to act out of inner conviction. Only God can do this, since He alone scrutinizes and judges the secret counsels of the heart." [58]

Religious freedom is a human freedom in the external forum of society. It is a personal and corporate right to immunity from coercion by any legal or extralegal forces in the profession and practice of religion. This right is grounded in the law of nature— or, if you will, in the exigence of reason—which manifests itself, in today's social historical context, both through the mature personal consciousness which claims the right and also through the mature political consciousness which forbids the state to deny or diminish it. It is evident that John XXIII's whole discussion of human and civil rights, including religious freedom, is commanded by the historical consciousness, by a sense of man's "spiritual aspirations" (*animorum appetitiones*) [59] which reason approves as expressions of man's growing consciousness of his own self-in-society—or, if you will, his own personal and social nature.

This is not liberalist individualism or any sort of false personalism. The Pope's thought reveals the methodology of natural-law thinking at its best, both in ethics and in politics. For him, religious freedom is not some sort of Platonic idea that has had no history but has been always somehow "there," to be seen by anyone who cared to look at it. Religious freedom is the reasonable affirmation of the contemporary human consciousness. In the Second View, which is that of John XXIII, it is also an affirmation of the Christian consciousness that has become aware of the essential link between a government of limited powers (Pius XII's "system of government that will be more in accord with the dignity and freedom of the citizenry") and religious freedom as a juridical notion, a civil and human right, to be protected by a legal institution written into constitutional law (John XXIII's more consequent affirmation).

John XXIII's second contribution to the new statement of the question of religious freedom, and to its solution, lay in his tetradic diagram of the spiritual forces that sustain human society: Leo XIII had endlessly reiterated the triad—truth, justice, and love; so too had Pius XII. John was the first Pope to add the fourth spiritual force, freedom, as coequally essential. The new tetrad was new; it was also fully traditional. The tradition has always asserted that the human quality of society depends on the freedom of the Church. In a new and more profound understanding of the tradition, John XXIII affirms that the human quality of society depends on the freedom of the people. The second juncture of ideas has been formally effected. In our age (the reiterated phrase in which John XXIII reveals his historical consciousness) the two freedoms are inseparable—in fact, they are identical. They stand or fall together. The doctrine of the Church affirms both of them. Her pastoral solicitude extends to each of them.

The spiritual order of society is founded on truth—on the true view of man, his dignity, his duties and rights, his freedoms and obligations. This order must be brought into being under fidelity to the precepts of justice, whose vindication is the primary function of the public power as well as the primary civic duty of the citizenry. This order needs to be animated and perfected by love; for civic unity cannot be achieved by justice and law alone; love is the ultimate force that sustains all human living together. Finally, this order is to achieve increasingly more human conditions of social equality, without any impairment of freedom.[60]

Truth, justice, and love assure the stability of society; but freedom is the dynamism of social progress toward fuller humanity in communal living.[61] The freedom of the people ranks as a political end, along with justice; it is a demand of justice itself. Freedom is also *the* political method whereby the people achieve their highest good, which is their own unity as a people: "A society of men achieves its unity (*coalescit*) by freedom, that is, by methods that are in keeping with the dignity of its citizens, who are by nature men of reason and who therefore assume responsibility for their own actions." [62] Society is bound to the usages or methods of freedom (*libertatis consuetudinem teneat*) [63] in its constant effort to base itself on truth, govern itself with justice, and permeate itself with civic friendship.

When the freedom of the people is unjustly limited,

the social order itself, which is an order of freedom, is overthrown. The problem of political refugees, for instance,

shows that the rulers of certain nations impose excessive limits on the just measure of freedom within which each citizen should be allowed to live a life worthy of a man. In fact, in this kind of state the very right to freedom is at times called into question or wholly denied. When this happens, the right order of civil society is overthrown in its very foundations; for by its nature the public power looks to the protection of the good of the community, and its chief duty is to recognize the legitimate reaches of freedom and to keep inviolable the rights of freedom.[64]

By this accent on the freedom of the people, new in modern papal utterances, the historical problematic of the nineteenth century is completely dissolved. The rightful autonomy of the people, implicit in Leo XIII's statement of the dyarchy, has received explicit affirmation. In particular, the state of the question of religious freedom has been altered. The distinction which Leo XIII could not make has now been made—between religious freedom as a juridical notion and a legal institution in a free society, and the false ideology and the resultant form of political regime that once inspired the notion and the institution.[65] Now religious freedom has a new basis in each of the four dynamic spiritual forces that sustain society. It is an exigence of truth, justice, and civic friendship or love. In particular, it is acknowledged to be an integral element of the freedom of the people.

It is not now a question of tolerating the institution as a lesser evil. John XXIII is not enlarging the

[83]

hypothesis of the First View. He is quietly bidding good-bye to both thesis and hypothesis in the sense of the *opinio recepta*. He represents the present term of a new development of the genuine tradition, *eodem sensu, eademque sententia.* Now the Church positively affirms the validity of the institution of religious freedom. It embodies a civil and human right, personal and corporate. It also embodies a recognition by government of one of the "legitimate reaches of freedom" (*honestos libertatis fines*) [66] which are immune from restriction by any legal or extralegal force.

The Second View must undertake the task of showing that it is the traditional view—the view that represents a valid and necessary growth in the understanding of the tradition. The foregoing pages illustrate a way in which this task may be accomplished. There may be other ways.

★ 3 ★

The Issues

Only the beginnings of an effort to initiate an intramural dialogue on religious freedom were made in the second and third conciliar sessions, in the speeches in the conciliar aula, and later in the comments, criticisms, and emendations sent in to the Secretariat for the Promotion of Christian Unity. A few illustrations will show the difficulties involved in setting afoot a dialogue between the First and Second Views.

For instance, the First View asks the question, whether a man has a natural right to found a false religion. It answers the question in the negative and considers that it has dealt a mortal blow to the Second View. The trouble is that the Second View does not answer the question in the affirmative. In fact, it is not inclined to answer the question at all. In the manner of its asking, under complete abstraction from all historical reality, the question is irrelevant to the issue of religious freedom in its contemporary sense, which supposes a given historical-social-political context. Hence no dialogue ensues.

Again, the First View asks the question, whether error is to be granted the same rights as truth. It returns a negative answer and again considers that it has cut the ground from under the Second View. The trouble is that the Second View does not stand on this simplistic ground. It clarifies the question to mean, whether the public power may positively authorize the existence and dissemination of religious error on the same footing on which it positively authorizes the existence and dissemination of religious truth. To the question thus framed, it answers again that the question itself is irrelevant to the contemporary issue of religious freedom. What is more, the fallacy of the previous question, so called, appears. Is it in any sense the function of government to authorize the public existence of any religion, true or false? The answer is no.

To give an example, the first Amendment to the Constitution of the United States does not positively authorize the existence and propaganda of Jehovah's Witnesses. Fortunately too, it does not positively authorize the existence and propaganda of the Catholic Church—fortunately, for such an authorization by the public power would be a monstrous violation of the freedom of the Church, which neither requires nor tolerates any such authorization. The legal institution of religious freedom in its contemporary sense is not a positive authorization of either truth or error. This institution does not "grant" rights, that is, confer empowerments in the matter of religion. Its essential premise is that the public power is not competent to confer such empowerments. In other words, its essential premise is a denial of Proposition 39 of the *Syllabus*. The First Amendment is simply the recognition of an immunity. By it the people of the United States, inspired by the personal and political consciousness, declared that the free exercise of religion is to be immune from coercive restriction by the power of the state or by any power within society. The First Amendment is a limitation imposed by a free people on the public power; it is not an assertion of the power of the state over the people, in the sense of Continental sectarian Liberalism. The issue, whether error is to be granted the same rights as truth, simply does not arise. Hence again there is no dialogue.

For a final example, the First View asks the question, whether the erroneous conscience has rights in the public forum. To illustrate its negative answer, it gives an example. If I mistakenly think you owe me five dollars, does my erroneous conscience give me the right to demand five dollars from you? Again the Second View declares the question to be irrelevant. As for the example, it limps badly. First, it is taken from the sphere of juridical relations between men, as ruled by commutative justice, whereas religious freedom has to do with man's relation to God. What is more important, it confuses the notion of right as an empowerment and as an immunity. My erroneous conscience gives me no empowerment to demand from you money that you do not owe me. On the other hand, my religious conscience, whether erroneous or not, confers on me an immunity from coercion, whether legal or extralegal, within limits defined by the exigences of public order. Once again the dialogue dies.

In its turn, the Second View asks some questions. It inquires, for instance, whether the whole issue of human rights is to be argued on the premise that the nature of man is a historical nature, whose rational exigences manifest themselves progressively, under the impact of the continually changing social-political context, and in response to the growing personal and political consciousness. In the face of this question, the First View tends either to look blank or to launch the accusation that this is juridical modernism. In either case, there is no dialogue.

Again, in what concerns the interpretation of papal documents, the Second View asks the question (apropos of Leo XIII, for instance), is not the historical context of the document and its doctrinal, polemic, and pastoral intentions to be considered, with the result that particular assertions may be regarded as historically conditioned and therefore subject to further development in what concerns their manner of conception and statement, under altered circumstances and with the rise of new questions which affect the perspectives in which the truth is viewed. The First View replies that Leo XIII did indeed speak within a historical context but that his utterances transcended the context. What matters is what he said—the propositions that he put down on paper. These propositions stand forever, true, certain, and immutable. The Second View may urge the issue, citing the assertion of Pius XII that Boniface VIII's doctrine of the sun and the moon and the two swords was historically conditioned and is today archaistic.[67] In reply, the First View changes the subject, raising the issue of the doctrinal authority of papal encyclicals, with appropriate citations. This issue is important, but it would seem to suppose an answer to the prior question. Again the parties fail to join in dialogue.

At that, this abortive dialogue seems to indicate where the real issue lies. The First and Second View do not confront each other as affirmation confronts negation. Their differences are at a deeper level—indeed, at a level so deep that it would be difficult to go deeper. They represent the contemporary clash between classicism and historical consciousness. This, however, is a subject too vast to be dealt with here. It will be sufficient further to illustrate the clash by considering the objections that each view brings against the other.

The First View accuses the Second View of doctrinal errors—Liberalism and neo-Liberalism, subjectivism, relativism, indifferentism, Rousseauism, laicism, social and juridical modernism, humanistic personalism, existentialism, situation ethics, false irenicism. These, at any rate, were the accusations brought against the incomplete and badly organized version of the Second View that appeared in the original text of Chapter Five of the Decree on Ecumenism. And there were others. It is not difficult to show that all these accusations rest upon misunderstanding. The Second View needs only to explain itself in order to show that these accusations of doctrinal error are groundless.

The Second View is less harsh in its judgment. It does not accuse the First View of doctrinal errors but of theological fallacies.

The first is archaism—the fallacy which maintains

that the Church's understanding and manner of statement of her faith, and of doctrines of reason related to faith, can and ought to be halted in some particular stage, under denial of the possibility and legitimacy of further development. The first historic victim of the fallacy was Eusebius of Caesarea during the controversy over the new Nicene formula of the Church's faith in the Son and Word. The scriptural formulas, said he and the men around him, are definitive; it is not permitted to go beyond them. These men refused to consider the fact that Arius had asked a new question which could not be answered, without ambiguity, in scriptural formulas. Similarly, the First View would fix the doctrine of the Church on religious freedom in its nineteenth-century stage of conception and statement. It refuses to consider the fact that the state of the question has been altered and the nineteenth-century answer is inadequate.

Archaism therefore consists in the rejection, on principle, of the more recent synthesis or systematization, and in the effort to adhere or return to the synthesis or systematization of a prior age, which is judged to be simple and more pure. History has known scriptural archaism, in the original Protestant Reform; patristic archaism, in Baius and Jansenius; medieval archaism, in various kinds of Scholastic Talmudism. The First View is a sort of political archaism. As Boniface VIII's doctrine was archaistic after the emergence of the autonomous nation-state in the fifteenth century, so the First View is archaistic after the growth of the personal and political consciousness in the twentieth century. With this growth in man's understanding of himself as a free man in a free society, Catholic doctrine on religious freedom must likewise grow in its understanding of itself. Pius XII glimpsed the fact and reckoned with it in his doctrine on the juridical state, but he drew back, with his wonted caution, from its full implications. With all the penetration of his extraordinary insight, John XXIII saw the fact with full clarity. His insight found expression in his articulated concept of the freedom of the people as a political end and as *the* political method, and in the correlative concept of religious freedom as a necessary and integral element of the freedom of the people. What remains is simply the fuller conceptualization of religious freedom as a social faculty, a human and civil right (personal and corporate), and a legal institution. What remains too is the recognition that the First View is archaistic, because all sense of the personal and political consciousness is absent from it.

The second fallacy is misplaced abstractness; it is the contrary of the famous fallacy of misplaced concreteness, identified by Alfred North Whitehead. It is the fallacy which creates ideologies. On the face of it, the First View presents itself as a theory conceived with full abstractness, the pure creation of the *conscience survolante*. In fact, however, it is an apologetic for the nation-state of largely Catholic population which began to take shape, under more or less absolutist rule, in the post-Tridentine era, and then felt the religious and political shock of the French Revolution. This special kind of political-legal realization began to receive recognition in a series of concordats in the nineteenth century, of which the first was with the Kingdom of the

Two Sicilies in 1818. It is, of course, entirely legitimate to construct an argument in favor of this historical realization. However, the argument would have to be constructed as Leo XIII constructed it—with concreteness and complete historical realism. The fallacy enters when the Leonine argument is transposed into an abstract thesis which proposes an abstract "ideal instance" of constitutional law, per se and in principle obligatory on an abstraction called "the state."

Here is the neuralgic point in the intramural dialogue on religious freedom. It may be that the intramural segment of the dialogue is not the most important today, given the world-wide character of the problem. Nevertheless, the intramural dialogue has priority. Until it is conducted to a conclusion and a Catholic consensus takes form, the ecumenical dialogue is impossible and so too is the dialogue between Christian and non-Christian. It has often been pointed out that, if the First View stands as the immutable formulation of Catholic doctrine, the whole dialogue *ad extra* is cut off before it can begin.

It has been alleged that the Second View implies a rejection of the classic concept of the Catholic confessional state. In its generality, this allegation is false. Obviously, the "Catholic state" is not a univocal concept. This fact will be admitted by anyone who is familiar with political history and with the variant content of concordats. The concept covers a whole variety of historical realizations, from the *ancien régime* with its Gallicanized Union of Throne and Altar, to contemporary Portugal, in which (according to some jurists) there is a mode of separation of Church and state. Some of these historical realizations were sufficiently ambiguous. In any case, the whole issue needs to be argued with great care and with due regard for all the necessary distinctions.

The primarily necessary distinction is between society (or the people) and state (or the order of public law and administration). From this distinction another follows immediately—between the public profession of religion by society (*officium religionis publicae*) and the care of religion by the public power (*cura religionis*). Neither of these distinctions is clearly and consistently maintained by Leo XIII. The result has been confusion.

Obviously, the Second View acknowledges, in common with all Catholics, that an obligation to profess faith in God and to worship Him is incumbent on society—on the people as such as well as on individuals. This obligation, however, is not fulfilled by legislative or executive action by the public power. It is fulfilled by occasional public acts of worship, usually on so-called state-occasions—the opening of the legislature and judiciary, national days of thanksgiving and prayer, etc. These acts of worship are organized by the Church, not by the government, which has no competence in liturgical matters. Moreover, they are to be voluntary acts, since they are formally acts of religion. No legal coercion may be exerted to force either individuals or the people to participate in these occasional acts of public faith and worship. All this is clear. The Second View rejects the sectarian Liberalist notion of religion as a purely private affair, against which Leo XIII insisted on the *officium religionis publicae*.

[93]

Obviously too, the Second View embraces the notion of the Christian society, described in the modern papal encyclicals. The development of the Christian social conscience is a duty of the highest order; so too is the effort to permeate all the institutions of society—economic, social, cultural, political—with the Christian spirit of truth, justice, love, and freedom; so too is the growth of the personal and political consciousness among the people. The helpless and inert *imperita multitudo* of Leo XIII's time was not a Christian people in the high sense of the word. The Second View rejects the notion of the laicized society in the sense of Continental sectarian Liberalism. In particular, it regards the religious unity of a particular society or people as a good of the highest order—an order so high that it transcends the political order. The emergence of such Catholic societies in history has been a work of divine providence. All this too is clear.

The difficulty begins when the distinct constitutional issue of public care of religion arises, scil., the function of the public power with regard to religion in society and among the people. Only here does the issue of the "Catholic state" become controversial. The word "state" has its proper political-legal meaning.

The First View maintains that there is an abstract idea of the order of constitutional law and an abstract idea of the religious competence of the public power that are distinctively Catholic. In this abstract conception, the Catholic order of constitutional law contains two related institutions, first, the establishment of Catholicism by law as the single religion of the state (i.e., the one religion recognized by law, which alone has the civil right of public existence, guaranteed and supported by the power of the state), and second, intolerance of other religions (i.e., the empowerment of the state to use its legal and police powers to exterminate from public existence all other religions). These twin institutions are of the legal order, matters of constitutional law. Establishment is not a profession of faith in the Catholic religion as the one true religion. It is a legal enactment whose force is felt in the public life of the people. Establishment is not an act of religion; it is a political act of the public power. (Historically, it normally found its place in the *constitution octroyée,* so called, which was not in any sense an act of the people but only of the ruler.) Moreover, the First View maintains that these two legal institutions, establishment and intolerance, constitute the "ideal instance" of constitutional law. Where they exist, the ideal "Catholic state" exists.

The ideal may be seen, for instance, in the Concordat with the Republic of Ecuador (September 26, 1862): "The Catholic Apostolic Roman religion shall continue to be the single (*única*) religion of the Republic of Ecuador, and it shall always be maintained in the possession of all the rights and prerogatives which it ought to enjoy according to the law of God and the dispositions of canon law. In consequence, no other dissident cult and no society condemned by the Church can ever be permitted in Ecuador."

Under allowance for some differences of opinion among its proponents, the general position of the Second View may be stated in the following five propositions.

1) It is not at all incompatible with the doctrine and practice of religious freedom that there should exist an "orderly relationship" (*ordinata colligatio,* in Leo XIII's phrase) between the public power, as the representative of the people, and the Church, which has authority over the community of the faithful. Moreover, this relationship may be made formally legal by a concordat. (A concordat would normally require ratification by the elected legislature in democratically organized countries, since it is an international convention.) Furthermore, out of respect for historical custom, where it exists, it is not inappropriate or contrary to religious freedom that the people of a particular nation should declare their common allegiance to the Catholic Church in some sort of constitutional document. This declaration has no juridical consequences; it has the value of a statement of fact.

2) In order that the relationship between the two powers may be orderly, the requirements of religious freedom must be observed. There are three.

First, there must be no infringement or inhibition of the freedom of the Church as a spiritual authority and as the community of the faithful. Her internal autonomy must remain inviolable and the free exercise of her apostolic mission must be unimpeded. Moreover, the Church is not to be used by the public power as *instrumentum regni.*

Second, there must be no confusion of the religious and the political—in particular, no confusion of religious unity and political unity. As the public power has no share whatever in the care of souls (*cura animarum*) or in the control of thought (*regimen animo-*

rum),[68] so it has no share whatever in the care of the unity of the Church. The unity of the Church is a unity of the supernatural order; the care of it is committed exclusively to the Church, and this care is to be exercised by the purely spiritual means proper to the Church. Even when the theological concept of the unity of the Church is historicized or temporalized to mean the religious unity of a given people or ethnic group in the one true faith, this fact must imply no politicization of the national Church, no empowerment of the state to protect or promote the unity of the national Church by coercive means. This would be an infringement of the freedom of the Church and a violation of the exigences of the Leonine dyarchy; it would also be action *ultra vires* by the public power. Moreover, the functions of the state with regard to the national culture, whatever they may be, imply no empowerment of the state with regard to the religious welfare of the people, which remains exclusively the duty and prerogative of the Church.

Third, the relationship between the Church and the national government must be so conceived and so executed that it will not result in the alienation of the people from the Church that was a prominent feature of the post-Tridentine and sectarian Liberalist eras. This would be, in effect, an infringement of the freedom of the Church as the community of the faithful.

3) The legal institution of religious intolerance is incompatible with religious freedom as an integral element of the freedom of the people. The right to religious freedom, personal and corporate (in the sense described above), is a rational exigence of the con-

[97]

temporary personal and political consciousness. The correlative exigence is that the public power should have no empowerment to use coercive measures to exterminate any religion from public existence and public action. Exceptions to this rule occur only in particular cases in which there is a clear violation of public order which makes demonstrably necessary the intervention of the public power. Moreover, this third proposition is not hypothesis in the sense of the First View. It is a matter of principle—theological, ethical, political, legal, jurisprudential. It is not a lamentably necessary concession to *force majeure,* made in order to avoid a greater evil or to gain a greater good. Religious freedom is a personal and political good. It is part of that "establishment of freedom" which, as Acton said and John XXIII in effect repeated, represents the "highest phase of civil society."

4) There is no such thing as an "ideal instance" of Catholic constitutional law. In particular, the twin institutions of establishment and intolerance do not represent the ideal instance. There may be some constitutional orders which are good and others which are bad. The first Catholic criterion of judgment was proposed by Pius XII, scil., whether the constitutional order assures the Church a stable condition in law and in fact and full freedom in the fulfilment of her spiritual ministry. (The centrality of the freedom of the Church is visible in the new series of concordats initiated by the Concordat with Latvia in 1922.) The second Catholic criterion was proposed by John XXIII, scil., whether the constitutional order assures the citizen the secure possession of all his personal rights and

protects and promotes in full measure the legitimate freedom of the people.

These two criteria are to base the Catholic judgment, no matter what may be the religious composition of the citizenry—whether conditions of religious unity or conditions of religious pluralism obtain. There are not two standards of judgment on constitutional law— one for a Catholic people and another for a religiously pluralist people. The fact of the religious unity of a particular people in the Catholic faith does not make obligatory the legal institution of establishment, as if a situation of legal privilege were a Catholic constitutional ideal. Still less does the religious unity of the people authorize the legal institution of intolerance, as if this institution were also a Catholic ideal.

In its turn, the Second View does not propose the legal institution of religious freedom as a constitutional ideal, an abstract thesis, conceived a priori, under abstraction from historical-social reality. It discards the categories of the ideal and the tolerable, thesis and hypothesis, as invalid categories of discussion about constitutional law. It goes back to the Jurist for its category of legal discussion. It is the function of law, said the Jurist, to be useful to the people.[69] Its categories of political discussion are taken from John XXIII—truth, justice, love, and the freedom of the people. As for its category of socio-religious discourse, it would prefer to abandon the ambiguous neologism, "the Catholic state," and go back to the noble medieval phrase, "the Christian people." This is not archaism; it is *ressourcement*.

5) As the historical consciousness precludes the fal-

lacy of archaism, so also it precludes the fallacy of anachronism. This latter fallacy consists in the assumption that a later and more perfect stage in the Church's understanding of her own tradition existed before it actually did exist. The Second View presents itself as the contemporary stage in the growing understanding of the tradition. This understanding cannot be found in ecclesiastical documents of the nineteenth century. It was brought into being by a dynamism proper to the twentieth century, the growth of the personal and political consciousness, first noted by Pius XII and more fully developed in its implications by John XXIII. The notion of religious freedom as a human and civil right, personal and corporate, is not to be sought in theologians of the nineteenth century, since it is explicitly the product of a twentieth-century insight into the exigences of the personal and political consciousness. The link between religious freedom and limited constitutional government, and the link between the freedom of the Church and the freedom of the people— these were not nineteenth-century theological-political insights. They became available only within twentieth-century perspectives, created by the "signs of the times." The two links were not forged by abstract deductive logic but by history, by the historical advance of totalitarian government, and by the corresponding new appreciation of man's dignity in society.

The complex notion of the freedom of the Church had indeed always stated the question of public care of religion in its proper terms. It had also stated the essential claim that the Church perennially must make on the public power, as the essential requirement of positive divine law that is binding on the public power. But the tradition had been obscured by history—by the decadence of the constitutional tradition after the *quattrocento* broke with the medieval conception of kingship, and by the involvement of the Church in the politics and power struggles of the late medieval period, the post-Tridentine era, and the century of sectarian Liberalism in Europe and Latin America.

However, what history had obscured, history would also clarify. History brought forth Proposition 39 of the *Syllabus,* brutally incarnate in a form of totalitarian society-state. In the light of history Leo XIII began to restate the question of public care of religion in its traditional terms and to restore the traditional central-ity of the Church's ancient claim to freedom in the face of the public power. Pius XI and Pius XII began to work out the wider political implications of the tradi-tion in the altered historical context of the twentieth century. By his fuller acceptance of the context, John XXIII renounced all archaism, confirmed the new problematic of religious freedom, and began to apply to its resolution the newly developed tradition, theologi-cal and political.

If archaism is now forbidden, so too is anachronism. The rejection of this latter fallacy controls the thought of the Second View in two major ways.

First, it controls the interpretation of papal docu-ments of the past. The Second View does not search in the Leonine corpus or elsewhere for "proof-texts," that is, for explicit earlier statements that will textually confirm the explicitness of its own later statements. Nor does it undertake to "read back" into the text of

Leo XIII its own synthesis of the tradition. Both of these procedures would be vitiated by anachronism, a violation of good theological method. As Leo XIII cannot be "read back" into Innocent III, so John XXIII cannot be "read back" into Leo XIII.

The theological task is to trace the stages in the growth of the tradition as it makes its way through history. Scylla is archaism; Charybdis is anachronism. The task is to discern the elements of the tradition that are embedded in some historically conditioned synthesis that, as a synthesis, has become archaistic. The further task is to discern the "growing end" of the tradition; it is normally indicated by the new question that is taking shape under the impact of the historical movement of events and ideas. There remains the problem of synthesis—of a synthesis that will be at once new and also traditional. This is the problem faced by the Second View.

Second, the rejection of anachronism controls judgments on past situations. To return to the example already given, the Second View does not denounce the Church or the Republic of Ecuador for a violation of religious freedom in 1862. More in general, in judging all past or present realizations of the Catholic state, so called, the historical situation needs to be considered. The historical institutions of establishment and intolerance are to be judged *in situ*. They might well be judged valid *in situ*. The function of law, said the Jurist, is to be useful to the people. These institutions might well have been useful to the people, in the condition of the personal and political consciousness of the people at the time. This was Leo XIII's judgment. It would be anachronistic to question it.

But if anachronism is outlawed, so too is archaism. Leo XIII himself rejected the latter fallacy by his restatement of the Gelasian dyarchy and the Gregorian principle of the freedom of the Church. It may still be useful for the people of God in certain countries of the world today that the Church should be recognized by law as the common religion of the people. This would validate the judgment that the institution of establishment should be retained in those countries. But nothing can validate the judgment that this legal status is "ideal" because it enlists the coercive power of government in the service of the exclusive rights of truth. To say the least, this view is archaistic. The argument would have to be that establishment is useful for assuring the freedom of the Church, as the people of God and as a spiritual authority. This argument might be more difficult to make. In any case, its conclusion would not be that establishment is a constitutional ideal.

On the other hand, no argument can be made today that would validate the legal institution of religious intolerance, much less canonize it as a Catholic ideal. The institution cannot even be tolerated today as a harmless archaism. Nor is it even permissible to raise the question, whether legal intolerance may be useful to the people—either to the people of God or to the civil people. The fact is that legal intolerance stands condemned today by the common consciousness of the peoples of the world. The condemnation is binding today on all civilized states, which, as such, must reject Proposition 39 of the *Syllabus*. Today, religious freedom, as a human and civil right, personal and corporate, which requires the protection of a legal institution, has emerged as an exigence of the personal and political reason. As such, it claims the sanction of Catholic doctrine.

These five propositions suggest the position taken by most proponents of the Second View with regard to the complicated issue of the "Catholic state," so called.

It is now possible to state the issues in the controversy.

There seems to be a basic agreement between the First and Second Views that the controversy concerns the constitutional question, the technical question of public care of religion by the public power, as a theological, ethical, political, legal, and jurisprudential question. This antecedent agreement is important, since it rules out irrelevant issues. There are, for instance, a number of issues involved in the larger problem which is customarily called, not without some ambiguity, the problem of "Church and state." These issues, however, are not directly relevant to the narrower question of public care of religion. From the foregoing exposition it is clear that the First and Second Views, in dealing with this question, make affirmations that are either contradictory or contrary.

1) The state of the question.—Has it altered in consequence of a Christian discernment of the new signs of the times (the Second View), or is it somehow by definition immutable (the First View)? This question seems to have first priority. Unless there can be

agreement on the state of the question, further argument is futile. Moreover, all other disagreements seem to stem from this one.

2) The basic concept in the question of public care of religion.—Is it the exclusive rights of truth (the First View) or the freedom of the Church as inseparably allied, in the present moment of history, with the freedom of the civil people (the Second View)?

3) Public care of religion in constitutional law.—Is there an ideal instance of Catholic constitutional law (the First View), or not (the Second View)? Furthermore, is there a dual standard for Catholic judgment on orders of constitutional law, one for the Catholic nation and another for religiously pluralist peoples (the First View), or is there a single standard equally applicable to any order of constitutional law (the Second View)? More in particular, are the categories of judgment the ideal and the tolerable, thesis and hypothesis, principle and expediency (the First View), or are they the good and the bad, the just and the unjust, the more or less just and the more or less unjust (the Second View)?

4) The competence of the public power with regard to religion.—Does it extend to public care of religious truth (the First View), or is it limited to public care of religious freedom (the Second View)? Does it extend to a care for the Church herself—her doctrine, authority, prestige (the First View), or is it limited to a care for the freedom of the Church (the Second View)? Does it extend to a care for the religious unity of the people as related to their political unity (the First View), or is it limited to a care for the religious

freedom of the people as related to their civil and political freedom (the Second View)?

5) The rule of jurisprudence for repressive intervention by the public power in what concerns the free exercise of religion.—Is it the possibility of such intervention without serious disturbance of the public order (the First View), or is it the necessity of such intervention in order to maintain the essential exigences of the public order (the Second View)?

6) The state and positive divine law.—What is the essential requirement of positive divine law which is binding on the state, that is, on the public power? Is the public power bound to establish the Church by law as the one religion of the public power, that is, the one religion whose right to public existence and action is recognized by the public power (the First View), or is this a misunderstanding of the whole matter (the Second View)? On the other hand, is the essential requirement of positive divine law satisfied when the public power recognizes and protects the freedom of the Church (the Second View), or is this a minimalizing of the whole matter (the First View)?

7) The legal institution of intolerance.—Is it the logical and juridical consequence of the legal establishment of the Church, in such wise that the two institutions stand or fall together (the First View), or is it possible to maintain an organic and even a legal relationship between the Church and the public power, and at the same time abolish the legal institution of intolerance and introduce the legal institution of religious freedom (the Second View)? More in particular, what are the correct premises on which to validate the

legal institution of establishment? And are there today any premises on which the legal institution of intolerance can be validated?

8) The issue of the Catholic confessional state.—This issue runs through all the foregoing seven issues, in such wise that the answer to it will depend on the answers to them. Here one general question may be added. To what extent is this kind of state—that is, this conception of the order of constitutional law and this conception of the religious competence of the public power—the creation of post-Tridentine history, and to what extent is it the creation of transtemporal doctrine?

9) The issue of theological judgment.—Is the Second View infected with doctrinal errors (as the First View maintains), or is the First View infected with theological fallacies (as the Second View maintains)? How successfully does each View contend with the objections brought against it by the other?

The basic issues in the controversy seem to come to expression in the foregoing series of nine interrelated topics. The node of the controversy also appears. It is the notion of the ideal. This is the "fighting word." But is the fight necessary? The Second View fights against the notion, because public care of religion is a constitutional question; it has to do with legal institutions, to which the notion of an ideal is inapplicable. The First View fights for the notion, because public care of religion has to do with the maintenance of the religious unity of a Catholic people, which is an ideal. If this is the issue, it is no issue at all. The Second View can grant that the religious unity of a Catholic people is an ideal to be pursued. The First View need only

[107]

grant that the legal institutions of establishment and intolerance are not ideal means of pursuing it. In any event, until the false issue of the ideal is disposed of, there is little possibility of getting on with the real argument. The ideal has become a King Charles's head, or, if you will, a red herring across the trail.

There are also three other sets of issues that must be briefly mentioned.

1) Religious freedom, as a concept and as an affirmation.—Has the concept been adequately described? And has the affirmation of it been reasonably made in terms of argument, and theologically made in terms of a genuine growth in the understanding of the tradition? Many particular issues arise under this general topic.

2) The mode of argument for the validity of religious freedom as a human and civil right, embodied in a legal institution.—The basic issue here concerns the different mentalities with which the whole question of public care of religion is approached—the extrinsecist-abstract-logical-deductive-ahistorical mentality (the First View), and the historical consciousness (the Second View). The cognate issue concerns the development of doctrine concerning public care of religion. Has there been a genuine growth in the understanding of the tradition from Gelasius I to John XXIII (the Second View), or did the growth come to a stop at some determined stage (the First View)?

3) Certain theological principles and pastoral considerations that are relevant to the whole problem.— The general question is, which of the two Views more

adequately reckons with these principles and considerations.

First, religious divisions are not simply brute fact but theological fact. That is to say, the fact of them is inherent in the supernatural economy of salvation. The economy hangs suspended from the divine predilection and predestination; faith is a gift offered to man's freedom; the economy is a divine action that unrolls in time and space; the eschatological division (Mt 25:31–46) is prefigured in history; Christ did not come to bring peace but division (Lk 12:51–53). No historical-geographical realizations of Catholic unity escape this theological fact. Religious pluralism is theologically the human condition.

Second, there is the mode of God's governance of men—its disposition to "overlook" (Acts 17:30), its "forbearance" (Rom 3:26), its respect for human freedom, its adamant resistance to the "divine temptation," as it has been called—the temptation to coerce men for their own good (cf. Mt 4:7).

Third, there is the evangelical consciousness of the Church—the *pusillus grex,* the pilgrim Church which is "poor," that is, dependent only on spiritual means to win wayfaring man to herself; the missionary Church, forever engaged in a work of discernment, seeking in the historical succession of human cultures for their truly human elements, striving always to save the institutions of men by filling them with a content of truth, justice, love, and freedom; willing always to recognize the reality of human progress, despite its ambiguities.

Fourth, there is the fact of the great sin of our times

—carelessness and even contempt for the dignity of the human person and its birthright of freedom. Against this sin, the Church has sharpened her emphasis on man as the image of God and also enlarged her pastoral solicitude for human freedom.

Fifth, there is the contemporary need for ecumenical dialogue on the issue of religious freedom, and the further need for dialogue between Christian and non-Christian. For this dialogue the Church needs a common doctrine; she also needs a doctrine that can be made intelligible to the contemporary man of good will.

These considerations, and others too, are relevant to the question of judgment on the two Views. Which of them is more in consonance with these theological truths? Which of them better reflects the contemporary pastoral solicitudes of the Church?

★ Notes ★

(The present work appeared originally in *Theological Studies* 25 1964, 503–75.)

1 Apr. 17, 1964; *AAS* 56 (1964) 389.

2 *Ci riesce, AAS* 45 (1953) 788–89.

3 *Ibid.*

4 *Libertas, ASS* 20 (1887–88) 605.

5 *Ibid.*, p. 609.

6 *Pacem in terris, AAS* 55 (1963) 279.

7 *Ibid.*, p. 265.

8 Cf. *ibid.*, p. 260.

9 Cf. *ibid.*

10 Cf. A. F. Carrillo de Albornoz, *The Basis of Religious Liberty* (New York, 1963) esp. pp. 16–26, 155–62.

11 Cf. Leo XIII, *Sapientiae christianae, ASS* 22 (1889–90) 396.

12 *Polycraticus* 8, 17 (*PL* 199, 777).

13 Cf. J. Lecler, *Toleration and the Reformation* 2 (tr. T. L. Westow; London, 1960) 197, 235, 250, 253, 279, 355, 362, 377, 379, 400, 426.

14 Cf. *Syllabus*, prop. 3 (*DB* 1703).

15 Cf. *Syllabus*, prop. 39 (*DB* 1739).

16 *Libertas, ASS* 20 (1887) 605.

17 *Immortale Dei, ASS* 18 (1885) 163.

18 *Libertas, ASS* 20 (1887) 605.

19 Cf. *ibid.*, p. 604.

20 Cf. *DB* 1800.

21 Cf. *Cum multa, ASS* 15 (1882) 242.

22 *Officio sanctissimo, ASS* 20 (1887) 269.

23 *Praeclara gratulationis, ASS* 26 (1893–94) 712.

24 *Immortale Dei, ASS* 18 (1885) 171.

25 *Libertas, ASS* 20 (1887) 612.

26 *Divini redemptoris, AAS* 29 (1937) 72.

27 Radiomessage, Dec. 24, 1944; *AAS* 37 (1945) 11–12.

28 *Ibid.*, p. 22.

29 Radiomessage, Dec. 24, 1942; *AAS* 35 (1943) 19.

30 *Ibid.*, p. 14.

31 Radiomessage, Dec. 24, 1944; *AAS* 37 (1945) 12.

32 *Ibid.*, p. 15.

33 Radiomessage, June 1, 1941; *AAS* 33 (1941) 200.

34 *Ibid.*

35 Cf. Radiomessage, Dec. 24, 1944; *AAS* 37 (1945) 13–16.

36 *Non abbiamo bisogno, AAS* 23 (1931) 302.

37 *Firmissimam constantiam, AAS* 29 (1937) 196.

38 *Summi pontificatus, AAS* 31 (1939) 445.

39 *Ci riesce, AAS* 45 (1953) 802.

40 *Mit brennender Sorge, AAS* 29 (1937) 160.

41 *Ibid.*, p. 159.

42 Radiomessage, Dec. 24, 1942; *AAS* 35 (1943) 19.

43 *AAS* 45 (1953) 794–802.

44 Cf. *ibid.*, p. 798.

45 *Ibid.*, p. 797.

46 *Ibid.*, p. 799.

47 *Ibid.*

48 *Ibid.*

49 *Ibid.*, pp. 798–99.

50 Cf. *ibid.*, p. 801.

51 Cf. *ibid.*, p. 797.

52 Radiomessage, Sept. 11, 1962; *AAS* 54 (1962) 682.

53 *AAS* 55 (1963) 257–304.

54 Cf. *ibid.*, pp. 273–79.

55 Cf. *ibid.*, p. 278.

56 Cf. *ibid.*, pp. 259–69.

57 *Ibid.*, p. 260.

58 *Ibid.*, p. 270.

59 *Ibid.*, p. 279.

60 *Ibid.*, p. 266.

61 Cf. *ibid.*, p. 265.

62 *Ibid.*, p. 266.

63 *Ibid.*, p. 297.

64 *Ibid.*, pp. 285–86.

65 Cf. *ibid.*, p. 300.

66 *Ibid.*

67 Cf. Allocution *Vous avez voulu*, Sept. 7, 1955; *AAS* 47 (1955) 678.

68 Cf. Leo XIII, *Sapientiae christianae, ASS* 22 (1889–90) 396.

69 Cf. 1–2, q. 95, a. 3.